THE OPEN DOOR

THE OPEN DOOR

When Writers First Learned to Read

STEVEN GILBAR

PREFACE BY BARBARA BUSH

Afterword by John Y. Cole

DAVID R. GODINE, PUBLISHER, INC.
in association with
THE CENTER FOR THE BOOK
in the Library of Congress

First published in 1989 by
D A V I D   R .   G O D I N E ,   P U B L I S H E R ,   I N C .
Horticultural Hall
300 Massachusetts Avenue
Boston, Massachusetts 02115

LIBRARY OF CONGRESS CATALOGING-IN-PUBLICATION DATA
The Open door : when writers first learned to read / selected by
Steven Gilbar.—1st ed.
p.   cm.
Includes bibliographical references.
ISBN 0-87923-809-7
1. Books and reading—United States. 2. Authors, American—Books and
reading. 3. Authors, English—Books and reading. 4. Books and reading—
Great Britain. 5. Authors, American—Biography—Youth. 6. Authors,
English—Biography—Youth. I. Gilbar, Steven.
Z1003.2.063 1989   89-45386
028'.9'0973—dc20   CIP

Photo Credits

Ben Franklin/Library of Congress; *William Cobbett*/Library of Congress; *Charles Dickens*/Library of Congress; *Frederick Douglass*/Library of Congress; *Abraham Cahan*/American Jewish Historical Society; *Rudyard Kipling*/The Bettmann Archive/BBC Hulton; *W. B. Yeats*/The Bettmann Archive/BBC Hulton; *H. G. Wells*/The Bettmann Archive/BBC Hulton; *Gertrude Stein*/UPI/Bettmann Newsphotos; *Winston Churchill*/The Bettmann Archive; *Sherwood Anderson*/The Bettmann Archive, Inc.; *Upton Sinclair and son*/The Bettmann Archive, Inc.; *H. L. Mencken*/UPI/Bettmann Newsphotos; *A. A. Milne and wife*/UPI/Bettmann Newsphotos; *Will Durant and wife*/UPI/Bettmann Newsphotos; *E. E. Cummings*/The Bettmann Archive; *Jean Rhys*/Pearl Freeman; *C. S. Lewis*/The Bettmann Archive/BBC Hulton; *John Steinbeck and wife*/UPI/Bettmann Newsphotos; *Isaac Bashevis Singer*/Layle Silbert; *Richard Wright* (left)/UPI/Bettmann Newsphotos; *M. F. K. Fisher*/Jill Krementz; *Eudora Welty*/Bettmann Newsphotos; *Dylan Thomas*/The Bettmann Archive/BBC Hulton; *"Harper Lee"*/Library of Congress; *Richard Rodriguez*/Robert Messick; *Stephen King*/Thomas Victor; *Annie Dillard*/The Dillard Family

First edition
PRINTED IN THE UNITED STATES OF AMERICA

*F*ew *things in life are as important as being able to read.*
1989—The Year of the Young Reader, a national campaign
initiated by the Library of Congress, encourages young people
to love books and reading. Schools, libraries, volunteer or-
ganizations, parents, and corporations around the country are
sponsoring hundreds of projects that introduce children to read-
ing at the earliest possible age.

What can you do? Share a book with a child. Read aloud,
and talk about what you read. Give a child a magazine
subscription. Take a young friend to a library or a bookstore;
both are wonderful places for opening up a young mind—
forever!

Barbara Bush
Honorary Chairperson
1989—The Year of the Young Reader

Contents

CONTENTS

THE OPEN DOOR

Benjamin Franklin

Benjamin Franklin
1706–1790

ENJAMIN FRANKLIN *was born in Boston, the fifteenth child of his father, a tallow chandler-soap maker. His early appetite for books led to a lengthy process of self-education. After serving as an apprentice printer to an older brother, Franklin moved to Philadelphia to establish his own printing business and publish his famous* Poor Richard's Almanack *and, later, the* Pennsylvania Gazette, *which became the* Saturday Evening Post. *He is best known in literature for his* Autobiography, *not fully published until 1868. His combination of talents—Franklin was writer, statesman, natural philosopher, scientist and printer—mark him as a versatile Man of the Enlightenment.*

From a child I was fond of reading, and all the little money that came into my hands was ever laid out in books. Pleased with the *Pilgrim's Progress*, my first collection was of John Bunyan's works in separate little volumes. I afterward sold them to enable me to buy R. Burton's *Historical Collections*; they were small chapmen's books, and cheap, forty or fifty in all. My father's little library consisted chiefly of books in polemic divinity, most of which I read, and have since often regretted that, at a time when I had such a thirst for knowledge, more proper books had not fallen in my way, since it was now resolved I should not be a clergyman. Plutarch's *Lives* there was in which I read abundantly, and I still think that time spent to great advantage. There was also a book of

De Foe's, called an *Essay on Projects*, and another of Dr. Mather's called *Essays to do Good*, which perhaps gave me a turn of thinking that had an influence on some of the principal future events of my life.

This bookish inclination at length determined my father to make me a printer, though he had already one son (James) of that profession. In 1717 my brother James returned from England with a press and letters to set up his business in Boston. I liked it much better than that of my father, but still had a hankering for the sea. To prevent the apprehended effect of such an inclination, my father was impatient to have me bound to my brother. I stood out some time, but at last was persuaded, and signed the indentures when I was yet but twelve years old. I was to serve as an apprentice till I was twenty-one years of age, only I was to be allowed journey-man's wages during the last year. In a little time I made great proficiency in the business, and became a useful hand to my brother. I now had access to better books. An acquaintance with the apprentices of booksellers enabled me sometimes to borrow a small one, which I was careful to return soon and clean. Often I sat up in my room reading the greatest part of the night, when the book was borrowed in the evening and to be returned early in the morning, lest it should be missed or wanted.

And after some time an ingenious tradesman, Mr. Matthew Adams, who had a pretty collection of books, and who frequented our printing-house, took notice of me, invited me to his library, and very kindly lent me such books as I chose to read. I now took a fancy to poetry, and made some little pieces; my brother, thinking it might turn to account, en-couraged me, and put me on composing occasional ballads. One was called *The Lighthouse Tragedy*, and contained an account of the drowning of Captain Worthilake, with his two daughters; the other was a sailor's song, on the taking of

Teach (or Blackbeard) the pirate. They were wretched stuff, in the Grub-street-ballad style; and when they were printed he sent me about the town to sell them. The first sold wonderfully, the event being recent, having made a great noise. This flattered my vanity; but my father discouraged me by ridiculing my performances, and telling me verse-makers were generally beggars. So I escaped being a poet, most probably a very bad one.

From *The Autobiography of Benjamin Franklin,* 1868

William Cobbett

William Cobbett
1763?–1835

 HE MAN G. K. Chesterton described as "the noblest English example of the noble calling of agitator" was born in Farnham, Surrey, the son of a farmer. After he published an incendiary political pamphlet in 1792, Cobbett fled to the United States and settled in Philadelphia for eight years, during which time he began writing social and political journalism under the name "Peter Porcupine." On his return to England in 1800 he founded Cobbett's Political Register, *which flourished for over thirty years. In 1832 Cobbett was elected to Parliament where he became a member of the Radical minority.*

At eleven years of age my employment was clipping of box-edgings and weeding beds of flowers in the garden of the Bishop of Winchester, at the Castle of Farnham. I had always been fond of beautiful gardens; and, a gardener, who had just come from the King's gardens at Kew, gave such a description of them as made me instantly resolve to work in these gardens. The next morning, without saying a word to any-body, off I set, with no clothes, except those upon my back, and thirteen halfpence in my pocket. I found that I must go to Richmond, and I, accordingly, went on, from place to place, inquiring my way thither. A long day (it was in June) brought me to Richmond in the afternoon. Two pennyworth of bread and cheese and a pennyworth of small beer, which I had on the road, and one halfpenny that I had lost somehow or other, left three pence in my pocket. With this for my whole fortune, I was trudging through Richmond in my blue smock-frock and my red garters tied under my knees, when, staring about me, my eye fell upon a little book, in a book-seller's window: *Tale of a Tub*; price 3*d*. The title was so odd, that my curiosity was excited. I had the 3*d*., but, then, I could have no supper. In I went and got the little book, which I was so impatient to read, that I got over into a field, at the upper corner of Kew Gardens, where there stood a haystack. On the shady side of this, I sat down to read. The book was so different from anything that I had ever read before: it was something so new to my mind, that, though I could not at all understand some of it, it delighted me beyond description; and it produced what I have always con-sidered a sort of birth of intellect. I read on till it was dark, without any thought about supper or bed. When I could see no longer, I put my little book in my pocket, and tumbled down by the side of the stack, where I slept till the birds in Kew Garden awaked me in the morning; when off I started to Kew, reading my little book. The singularity of my dress, the simplicity of my manner, my confident and lively air, induced the gardener, who was a Scotchman, I remember, to give me victuals, find me lodging, and set me to work. And, it was during the period that I was at Kew, that the King and two of his brothers laughed at the oddness of my dress, while I was sweeping the grass plat round the foot of the Pagoda. The gardener, seeing me fond of books, lent me some gardening books to read; but, these I could not relish after my *Tale of a Tub*, which I carried about with me wher-ever I went, and when I, at about twenty years old, lost it in a box that fell overboard in the Bay of Funday in North America, the loss gave me greater pain than I have ever felt at losing thousands of pounds.

From *The Autobiography of William Cobbett:*
The Progress of a Ploughboy to a Seat in Parliament, 1933

Charles Dickens

1812–1870

ORN INTO *a "shabby genteel" family of Portsea on the southern coast of England, the young Dickens moved about with his family until finally settling in a poor neighborhood in London. His childhood was unhappy, and like some of the less fortunate characters in his novels, his family's economic conditions forced Dickens to work in a factory at the age of twelve. At the pinnacle of his success Dickens wrote: "It is wonderful to me how I could have been so easily cast away at such an age. . . . My whole nature was so penetrated with grief and humiliation of such considerations, that even now, famous and caressed and happy, I often forget in my dreams that I have a dear wife and children; even that I am a man; and wander desolately back to that time of my life." During this time he, like the young hero of his famous novel,*
David Copperfield, *found escape in books.*

It was this. My father had left a small collection of books in a little room upstairs, to which I had access (for it adjoined my own) and which nobody else in our house ever troubled. From that blessed little room, Roderick Random, Peregrine Pickle, Humphrey Clinker, Tom Jones, the Vicar of Wakefield, Don Quixote, Gil Blas, and Robinson Crusoe, came out, a glorious host, to keep me company. They kept alive my fancy, and my hope of something beyond that place and time,—they, and the *Arabian Nights*, and the *Tales of the Genii*,—and did me no harm; for whatever harm was in some

Charles Dickens

of them was not there for me; *I* knew nothing of it. It is astonishing to me now, how I found time, in the midst of my porings and blunderings over heavier themes, to read those books as I did. It is curious to me how I could ever have consoled myself under my small troubles (which were great troubles to me), by impersonating my favourite characters in them—as I did—and by putting Mr. and Miss Murdstone into all the bad ones—which I did too. I have been Tom Jones (a child's Tom Jones, a harmless creature) for a week together. I have sustained my own idea of Roderick Random for a month at a stretch, I verily believe. I had a greedy relish for a few volumes of Voyages and Travels—I forget what, now—that were on those shelves; and for days and days I can remember to have gone about my region of our house, armed with the centre-piece out of an old set of boot-trees—the perfect realization of Captain Somebody, of the Royal British Navy, in danger of being beset by savages, and resolved to sell his life at a great price. The Captain never lost dignity, from having his ears boxed with the Latin Grammar. I did; but the Captain was a Captain and a hero, in despite of all the grammars of all the languages in the world, dead or alive.

This was my only and my constant comfort. When I think of it, the picture always rises in my mind, of a summer evening, the boys at play in the churchyard, and I sitting on my bed, reading as if for life. Every barn in the neighbourhood, every stone in the church, and every foot in the churchyard, had some association of its own, in my mind, connected with these books, and stood for some locality made famous in them. I have seen Tom Pipes go climbing up the churchsteeple; I have watched Strap, with the knapsack on his back, stopping to rest himself upon the wicket-gate; and I *know* that Commodore Trunnion held that club with Mr. Pickle, in the parlour of our little village alehouse.

From *David Copperfield*, 1850

Frederick Douglass (seated) and son

Frederick Douglass
1817?–1895

HE FAMOUS black abolitionist, born a slave in Tuckahoe, Maryland, took the name Douglass—from Sir Walter Scott's hero in The Lady of the Lake—*after his second, and successful, attempt to escape from slavery in 1838. After publication of his remarkable autobiography,* Narrative of the Life of Frederick Douglass *(1845), he feared capture as a fugitive slave and fled to England and Ireland until English friends purchased his freedom. He established* The North Star *in Rochester, New York, and served as its editor for seventeen years. After the Civil War he continued to urge civil rights for blacks, and was appointed Recorder of Deeds of the District of Columbia and minister to Haiti.*

The frequent hearing of my mistress reading the Bible aloud, for she often read aloud when her husband was absent, awakened my curiosity in respect to this *mystery* of reading, and roused in me the desire to learn. Up to this time I had known nothing whatever of this wonderful art, and my ignorance and inexperience of what it could do for me, as well as my confidence in my mistress, emboldened me to ask her to teach me to read. With an unconscious and inexperience equal to my own, she readily consented, and in an incredibly short time, by her kind assistance, I had mastered the alphabet and could spell words of three or four letters. My mistress seemed almost as proud of my progress as if I had been her own child, and supposing that her husband would be as well pleased, she made no secret of what she was doing for me. Indeed, she exultingly told him of the aptness of her pupil and of her intention to persevere, as she felt it her duty to do, in teaching me, at least, to read the Bible. And here arose the first dark cloud over my Baltimore prospects, the precursor of chilling blasts and drenching storms. Master Hugh was astounded beyond measure and, probably for the first time proceeded to unfold to his wife the true philosophy of the slave system, and the peculiar rules necessary in the nature of the case to be observed in the management of human chattels. Of course he forbade her to give me any further instruction, telling her in the first place that to do so was unlawful, as it was also unsafe; "for," said he, "if you give a nigger an inch he will take an ell. Learning will spoil the best nigger in the world. If he learns to read the Bible it will forever unfit him to be a slave. He should know nothing but the will of his master, and learn to obey it. As to himself, learning will do him no good, but a great deal of harm, making him disconsolate and unhappy. If you teach him how to read, he'll want to know how to write, and this accomplished, he'll be running away with himself." Such was the tenor of Master Hugh's oracular exposition; and it must be confessed that he very clearly comprehended the nature and the requirements of the relation of master and slave. His discourse was the first decidedly anti-slavery lecture to which it had been my lot to listen. Mrs. Auld evidently felt the force of what he said, and like an obedient wife, began to shape her course in the direction indicated by him. The effect of his words *on me* was neither slight nor transitory. His iron sentences cold and harsh, sunk like heavy weights deep into my heart, and stirred up within me a rebellion not soon to be allayed.

This was a new and special revelation, dispelling a painful mystery against which my youthful understanding had struggled, and struggled in vain, to wit, the white man's power to perpetuate the enslavement of the black man. "Very well," thought I. "Knowledge unfits a child to be a slave." I instinctively assented to the proposition, and from that moment I understood the direct pathway from slavery to freedom. It was just what I needed, and it came to me at a time and from a source whence I least expected it. Of course I was greatly saddened at the thought of losing the assistance of my kind mistress, but the information so instantly derived to some extent compensated me for the loss I had sustained in this direction. Wise as Mr. Auld was, he underrated my comprehension, and had little idea of the use to which I was capable of putting the impressive lesson he was giving to his wife. He wanted me to be a slave; I had already voted against that on the home plantation of Col. Lloyd. That which he most loved I most hated; and the very determination which he expressed to keep me in ignorance only rendered me the more resolute to seek intelligence. In learning to read, therefore, I am not sure that I do not owe quite as much to the opposition of my master as to the kindly assistance of my amiable mistress. I acknowledge the benefit rendered me by the one, and by the other, believing that but for my mistress I might have grown up in ignorance.

From *Life and Times of Frederick Douglass*, 1881

Abraham Cahan

Abraham Cahan
1860–1951

OWHERE HAS *the Lower East Side of New York been better described than in Cahan's novel,* The Rise of David Levinsky *(1917). As a struggling immigrant, he worked in its tenements, taught in its schools, and was instrumental in organizing the early Jewish unions of the garment industry. He was the founder—and from 1902 to 1951 the editor—of its outstanding newspaper,* The Jewish Daily Forward. *Though David Levinsky is not Abraham Cahan, the similarities of their backgrounds makes the early part of the novel at least partly autobiographical. Unlike Cahan, David Levinsky had received no secular education until he came to America. One of the first things he did was to enroll in a public evening school.*

Evening school closed in April. The final session was of a festive character. Bender, excited and sentimental, distributed some presents.

"Promise me that you will read this glorious book from beginning to end, Levinsky," he said, solemnly, as he handed me a new volume of *Dombey and Son* and a small dictionary. "We may never meet again. So you will have something to remind you that once upon a time you had a teacher whose name was Bender and who tried to do his duty."

I wanted to thank him, to say something handsome, but partly because I was overcome by his gift, partly because I was at a loss for words, I merely kept saying, sheepishly, "Thank you, thank you, thank you, thank you."

That volume of Dickens proved to be the ruin of my push-cart business and caused me some weeks of the blackest misery I had ever experienced.

As I started to read the voluminous book I found it an extremely difficult task. It seemed as though it was written in a language other than the one I had been studying during the past few months. I had to turn to the dictionary for the meaning of every third word, if not more often, while in many cases several words in succession were Greek to me. Some words could not be found in my little dictionary at all, and in the case of many others the English definitions were as much of an enigma to me as the words they were supposed to interpret. Yet I was making headway. I had to turn to the dictionary less and less often.

It was the first novel I had ever read. The dramatic interest of the narrative, coupled with the poetry and the humor with which it is so richly spiced, was a revelation to me. I had had no idea that Gentiles were capable of anything so wonderful in the line of book-writing. To all of which should be added my self-congratulations upon being able to read English of this sort, a state of mind which I was too apt to mistake for my raptures over Dickens. It seemed to me that people who were born to speak this language were of a superior race.

I was literally intoxicated, and, drunkard-like, I would delay going to business from hour to hour. The upshot was that I became so badly involved in debt that I dared not appear with my push-cart for fear of scenes from my creditors. Moreover, I scarcely had anything to sell. Finally I disposed of what little stock I still possessed for one-fourth of its value, and, to my relief as well as to my despair, my activities as a peddler came to an end.

I went on reading, or, rather, studying *Dombey and Son* with voluptuous abandon till I found myself literally penniless.

I procured a job with a man who sold dill pickles to Jewish grocers. From his description of my duties—chiefly as his bookkeeper—I expected that they would leave me plenty of leisure, between whiles, to read my Dickens. I was mistaken. My first attempt to open the book during business hours, which extended from eight in the morning to bedtime, was suppressed. My employer, who had the complexion of a dill pickle, by the way, proved to be a severe taskmaster, absurdly exacting, and so niggardly that I dared not take a decent-looking pickle for my lunch.

From *The Rise of David Levinsky*, 1917

Rudyard Kipling

Rudyard Kipling
1865–1936

ORN IN *Bombay, Kipling spent half his childhood in India and half in England, where he endured five years of intense suffering in the tyrannical care of a foster home. In that harsh environment, books provided an escape from unhappiness. When he was seventeen he returned to India, where he soon made a reputation for himself as a journalist, poet and short-story writer. Eight years later he was back in England and achieved immediate success with the publication of his first novel,* The Light That Failed *(1890). From that point he produced a stream of verse and stories, including his popular works for children,* The Jungle Book *(1894) and* Just So Stories *(1902). In 1907, Kipling became the first Englishman to receive the Nobel Prize for literature.*

I was made to read without explanation, under the usual fear of punishment. And on a day that I remember it came to me that 'reading' was not 'the Cat lay on the Mat,' but a means to everything that would make me happy. So I read all that came within my reach. As soon as my pleasure in this was known, deprivation from reading was added to my punishments. I then read by stealth and the more earnestly.

There were not many books in that house, but Father and Mother as soon as they heard I could read sent me priceless volumes. One I have still, a bound copy of *Aunt Judy's Magazine* of the early 'seventies, in which appeared Mrs. Ewing's

Six to Sixteen. I owe more in circuitous ways to that tale than I can tell. I knew it, as I know it still, almost by heart. Here was a history of real people and real things. It was better than Knatchbull-Hugesson's *Tales at Tea-time*, better even than *The Old Shikarri* with its steel engravings of charging pigs and angry tigers. On another plane was an old magazine with Scott's "I climbed the dark brow of the mighty Helvellyn." I knew nothing of its meaning but the words moved and pleased. So did other extracts from the poems of "A. Tennyson."

A visitor, too, gave me a little purple book of severely moral tendency called *The Hope of the Katzekopfs*—about a bad boy made virtuous, but it contained verses that began, "Farewell Rewards and Fairies," and ended with an injunction "To pray for the 'noddle' of William Churne of Staffordshire." This bore fruit afterwards.

And somehow or other I came across a tale about a lion-hunter in South Africa who fell among lions who were all Freemasons and with them entered into a confederacy against some wicked baboons. I think that, too, lay dormant until the *Jungle Books* began to be born.

There comes to my mind here a memory of two books of verse about child-life which I have tried in vain to identify. One—blue and fat—described "nine white wolves" coming "over the wold" and stirred me to the deeps; and also certain savages who "thought the name of England was something that could not burn."

The other book—brown and fat—was full of lovely tales in stange metres. A girl was turned into a water-rat "as a matter of course"; an Urchin cured an old man of gout by means of a cool cabbage-leaf, and somehow "forty wicked Goblins" were mixed up in the plot; and a "Darling" got out on the house-leads with a broom and tried to sweep stars off the skies. It must have been an unusual book for that age, but I have never been able to recover it, any more than I have a song that a nursemaid sang at low-tide in the face of the sunset on Littlehampton Sands when I was less than six. But the impression of wonder, excitement and terror and the red bars of failing light is as clear as ever.

Among the servants in the House of Desolation was one from Cumnor, which name I associated with sorrow and darkness and a raven that "flapped its wings." Years later I identified the lines: "And thrice the Raven flapped her wing Around the towers of Cumnor Hall." But how and where I first heard the lines that cast the shadow is beyond me— unless it be that the brain holds everything that passes within reach of the senses, and it is only ourselves who do not know this.

From *Something of Myself: For Friends Known and Unknown,* 1937

W. B. Yeats

W. B. Yeats
1865–1939

ILLIAM BUTLER YEATS was born near Dublin, in Sandymount, into an Anglo-Irish Protestant family. He spent much of his childhood in Sligo, on Ireland's northwest coast, an area he would later evoke in his poetry. Although as a boy he was not a great reader, he was a great listener; Yeats once wrote: "I have remembered nothing that I read, but only those things I heard or saw." Today, he is generally regarded as one of the greatest poets of his period.

Because I had found it hard to attend to anything less inter-esting than my thoughts, I was difficult to teach. Several of my uncles and aunts had tried to teach me to read, and because they could not, and because I was much older than children who read easily, had come to think, as I have learnt since, that I had not all my faculties. But for an accident they might have thought so for a long time. My father was staying in the house and never went to church, and that gave me the courage to refuse to set out one Sunday morning. I was often devout, my eyes filling with tears at the thought of God and for my own sins, but I hated church. My grandmother tried to teach me to put my toes first to the ground because I suppose I stumped on my heels and that took my pleasure out of the way there. Later on when I had learnt to read I took pleasure in the words of the hymn, but never under-stood why the choir took three times as long as I did in getting to the end; and the part of the service I liked, the sermon and passages of the Apocalypse and Ecclesiastes, were no compensation for all the repetitions and for the fatigue of so much standing. My father said if I would not go to church he would teach me to read. I think now that he wanted to make me for my grandmother's sake and could think of no other way. He was an angry and impatient teacher and flung the reading-book at my head, and next Sunday I decided to go to church. My father had, however, got interested in teaching me, and only shifted the lesson to a weekday till he had conquered my wandering mind. My first clear image of him was fixed on my imagination, I believe, but a few days before the first lesson. He had just arrived from London and was walking up and down the nursery floor. He had a very black beard and hair, and one cheek bulged out with a fig that was there to draw the pain out of a bad tooth. One of the nurses (a nurse had come from London with my brothers and sisters) said to the other that a live frog, she had heard, was best of all. Then I was sent to a dame school kept by an old woman who stood us in rows and had a long stick like a billiard cue to get at the back rows. My father was still at Sligo when I came back from my first lesson and asked me what I had been taught. I said I had been taught to sing, and he said, "Sing then" and I sang

> Little drops of water,
> Little grains of sand,
> Make the mighty ocean,
> And the pleasant land

high up in my head. So my father wrote to the old woman that I was never to be taught to sing again, and afterwards other teachers were told the same thing. Presently my eldest sister came on a long visit and she and I went to a little two-storied house in a poor street where an old gentlewoman taught us spelling and grammar. When we had learned our lesson well, we were allowed to look at a sword presented to her father who had led troops in India or China and to spell out a long complimentary inscription on the silver scabbard. As we walked to her house or home again we held a large umbrella before us, both gripping the handle and guiding ourselves by looking out of a round hole gnawed in the cover by a mouse. When I had got beyond books of one syllable, I began to spend my time in a room called the Library, though there were no books in it that I can remember except some old novels I never opened and a many-volumed encyclopedia published towards the end of the eighteenth century. I read this encyclopedia a great deal and can remember a long passage considering whether fossil wood despite its appearance might not be only a curiously shaped stone.

My father read out poetry, for the first time, when I was eight or nine years old. Between Sligo and Rosses Point, there is a tongue of land covered with coarse grass that runs out into the sea or the mud according to the state of the tide. It is the place where dead horses are buried. Sitting there, my father read me *The Lays of Ancient Rome*. It was the first poetry that had moved me after the stable-boy's *Orange Rhymes*. Later on he read me *Ivanhoe* and *The Lay of the Last Minstrel*, and they are still vivid in the memory. I re-read *Ivanhoe* the other day, but it has all vanished except Gurth, the swineherd, at the outset and Friar Tuck and his venison pasty, the two scenes that laid hold of me in childhood. *The Lay of the Last Minstrel* gave me a wish to turn magician that competed for years with the dream of being killed upon the seashore. When I first went to school, he tried to keep me from reading boys' papers, because a paper, by its very nature, as he explained to me, had to be made for the average boy or man and so could not but thwart one's growth. He took away my paper and I had not courage to say that I was but reading and delighting in a prose retelling of the *Iliad*.

But after a few months, my father said he had been too anxious and became less urgent about my lessons and less violent if I had learnt them badly, and he ceased to notice what I read. From then on I shared the excitement which ran through all my fellows on Wednesday afternoons when the boys' papers were published, and I read endless stories I have forgotten as I have forgotten *Grimm's Fairy Tales* that I read at Sligo, and all of Hans Andersen except the "Ugly Duckling" which my mother had read to me and to my sisters. I remember vaguely that I liked Hans Andersen better than Grimm because he was less homely, but even he never gave me the knights and dragons and beautiful ladies that I longed for.

From *Reveries Over Childhood and Youth,* 1916

H. G. Wells
1866–1946

HE SON of a professional cricketer, Herbert George Wells grew up in Bromley, Kent. When he was twelve his father's financial problems became so serious that Wells was apprenticed to a draper. But a few years later he won a scholarship to study science and literature, to write essays, reviews, and textbooks. Soon after, he began to write science fiction novels, and with the publication of The Time Machine *in 1895, Wells began one of the most prolific and versatile literary careers of any modern writer.*

My leg was broken for me when I was between seven and eight. Probably I am alive to-day and writing this autobiography instead of being a worn-out, dismissed and already dead shop assistant, because my leg was broken. The agent of good fortune was "young Sutton," the grown-up son of the landlord of the *Bell.* I was playing outside the scoring tent in the cricket field and in all friendliness he picked me up and tossed me in the air. "Whose little kid are you?" he said, and I wriggled, he missed his hold on me and I snapped my tibia across a tent peg. A great fuss of being carried home; a painful setting—for they just set and strapped a broken leg tightly between splints in those days, and the knee and ankle swelled dreadfully—and then for some weeks I found myself enthroned on the sofa in the parlour as the most important thing in the house, consuming unheard-of jellies, fruits, brawn and chicken sent with endless apologies on

H. G. Wells

behalf of her son by Mrs. Sutton, and I could demand and
have a fair chance of getting anything that came into my
head, books, paper, pencils, and toys—and particularly
books.

I had just taken to reading. I had just discovered the art of
leaving my body to sit impassive in a crumpled up attitude
in a chair or sofa, while I wandered over the hills and far
away in novel company and new scenes. And now my father
went round nearly every day to the Literary Institute in
Market Square and got one or two books for me, and Mrs.
Sutton sent some books, and there was always a fresh book
to read. My world began to expand very rapidly, and when
presently I could put my foot to the ground, the reading
habit had got me securely. Both my parents were doubtful
of the healthiness of reading, and did their best to discourage
this poring over books as soon as my leg was better.

I cannot recall now many of the titles of the books I read,
I devoured them so fast, and the title and the author's name
in those days seemed a mere inscription on the door to delay
me in getting down to business. There was a work, in two
volumes, upon the countries of the world, which I think
must have been made of bound up fortnightly parts. It was
illustrated with woodcuts, the photogravure had still to come
in those days, and it took me to Tibet, China, the Rocky
Mountains, and forests of Brazil, Siam and a score of other
lands. I mingled with Indians and naked negroes; I learnt
about whaling and crossed the drift ice with Esquimaux.
There was Wood's *Natural History*, also copiously illustrated
and full of exciting and terrifying facts. I conceived a profound fear of the gorilla, of which there was a fearsome
picture, which came out of the book at times after dark and
followed me noiselessly about the house. The half landing
was a favourite lurking place for this terror. I passed it whis-
tling, but wary and then ran for my life up the next flight.

And I was glad to think that between the continental land masses of the world, which would have afforded an unbroken land passage for wolves from Russia and tigers from India, and this safe island on which I took my daily walks, stretched the impassable moat of the English Channel. I read too in another book about the distances of the stars, and that seemed to push the All Seeing Eye very agreeably away from me. Turning over the pages of the Natural History, I perceived a curious relationship between cats and tigers and lions and so forth, and to a lesser degree between them and hyenas and dogs and bears, and between them again and other quadrupeds, and curious premonitions of evolution crept into my thoughts. Also I read the life of the Duke of Wellington and about the American Civil War, and began to fight campaigns and battles in my reveries. At home were the works of Washington Irving and I became strangely familiar with Granada and Columbus and the Companions of Columbus. I do not remember that any story books figured during this first phase of reading. Either I have forgotten them or they did not come my way. Later on, however, Captain Mayne Reid, Fenimore Cooper and the Wild West generally, seized upon my imagination.

One important element in that first bout of reading was the bound volumes of *Punch* and its rival in those days, *Fun*, which my father renewed continually during my convalescence. The bound periodicals with their political cartoons and their quaint details played a curious part in developing my imaginative framework. My ideas of political and international relations were moulded very greatly by the big figures of John Bull and Uncle Sam, the French, the Austrian, and the German and Russian emperors, the Russian bear, the British lion and the Bengal tiger, Mr. Gladstone the noble, and the insidious, smiling Dizzy. They confronted one another; they said heroic, if occasionally quite incomprehensible things to one another. And across the political scene also marched tall and lovely feminine figures, Britannia, Erin, Columbia, La France, bare armed, bare necked, showing beautiful bare bosoms, revealing shining thighs, wearing garments that were a revelation in an age of flounces and crinolines. My first consciousness of women, my first stirrings of desire were roused by these heroic divinities.

From *Experiment in Autobiography:*
Discoveries and Conclusions of a Very Ordinary Brain, 1934

Gertrude Stein

Gertrude Stein
1874–1946

LTHOUGH SHE WAS born in Allegheny, Penn-sylvania, Gertrude Stein is often thought of as a European writer. Much of her childhood was spent in Vienna and Paris, and as an adult she became an expatriate and the focus of the most exclusive literary circles in Paris, spending the rest of her life in France. In The Autobiography of Alice B. Toklas *(1933), in which she pretends to see the world through the eyes of her longtime companion, Stein remembers in characteristic prose style when her "bookish life" began.*

Her bookish life commenced at this time. She read anything that was printed that came her way and a great deal came her way. In the house were a few stray novels, a few travel books, her mother's well bound books Wordsworth Scott and other poets, Bunyan's Pilgrim's Progress a set of Shake-speare with notes, Burns, Congressional Records encyclo-pedias etcetera. She read them all and many times. She and her brothers began to acquire other books. There was also the local free library and later in San Francisco there were the mercantile and mechanics libraries with their excellent sets of eighteenth century and nineteenth century authors. From her eighth year when she absorbed Shakespeare to her fifteenth year when she read Clarissa Harlowe, Fielding, Smollett et-cetera and used to worry lest in a few years more she would have read everything and there would be nothing unread to read, she lived continuously with the english language. She read a tremendous amount of history, she often laughs and says she is one of the few people of her generation that has read every line of Carlyle's Frederick the Great and Lecky's Constitutional History of England besides Charles Grandison and Wordsworth's longer poems. In fact she was as she still is always reading. She reads anything and everything and even now hates to be disturbed and above all however often she has read a book and however foolish the book may be no one must make fun of it or tell her how it goes on. It is still as it always was real to her.

From The Autobiography of Alice B. Toklas, 1933

Winston Churchill
1874–1965

 HURCHILL *is best known as the prime minister who rallied and led England during the Second World War. However, his relatively frequent periods out of office gave him an opportunity to cultivate his talent for biography and for contemporary history, that culminated in the Nobel Prize for literature in 1953. Churchill and his family lived in a house called "The Little Lodge" near young Winston's grandfather, the Viceroy. Here Churchill writes with humor about first being taught to read by his nanny, Mrs. Everest.*

It was at "The Little Lodge" I was first menaced with Education. The approach of a sinister figure described as "the Governess" was announced. Her arrival was fixed for a certain day. In order to prepare for this day Mrs. Everest produced a book called *Reading without Tears*. It certainly did not justify its title in my case. I was made aware that before the Governess arrived I must be able to read without tears. We toiled each day. My nurse pointed with a pen at the different letters. I thought it all very tiresome. Our preparations were by no means completed when the fateful hour struck and the Governess was due to arrive. I did what so many oppressed peoples have done in similar circumstances: I took to the woods. I hid in the extensive shrubberies—forests they seemed—which surrounded "The Little Lodge." Hours passed before I was retrieved and handed over to "the Governess." We continued to toil every day, not only at letters

Winston Churchill

but at words, and also at what was much worse, figures. Letters after all had only got to be known, and when they stood together in a certain way one recognised their formation and that it meant a certain sound or word which one uttered when pressed sufficiently. But the figures were tied into all sorts of tangles and did things to one another which it was extremely difficult to forecast with complete accuracy. You had to say what they did each time they were tied up together, and the Governess apparently attached enormous importance to the answer being exact. If it was not right, it was wrong. It was not any use being "nearly right." In some cases these figures got into debt with one another: you had to borrow one or carry one, and afterwards you had to pay back the one you had borrowed. These complications cast a steadily gathering shadow over my daily life. They took one away from all the interesting things one wanted to do in the nursery or in the garden. They made increasing inroads upon one's leisure. One could hardly get time to do any of the things one wanted to do. They became a general worry and preoccupation. . . .

From *My Early Life: A Roving Commission,* 1930

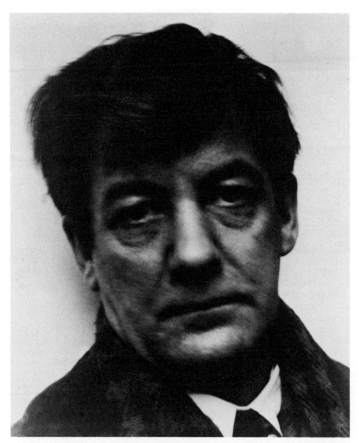

Sherwood Anderson

Sherwood Anderson
1876–1941

HE AUTHOR of Winesburg, Ohio *(1919) was born in Camden, Ohio, the third of seven children. His formal education ended at the age of fourteen, but his father was a door-to-door salesman of books, most of which he hungrily read. Anderson came to be a writer relatively late in life, quitting his job at a paint factory in 1912 in order to "sit with people, listen to words, tell tales of people, what they are thinking, what they are feeling." He went to Chicago, got caught up in the literary renaissance taking place there at that time, and quickly established himself as an important voice. Despite his late start, Anderson had a long and prolific writing career and later influenced such writers as Hemingway, Fitzgerald, and Faulkner.*

I read other books, any books I could get my hands on. I went fishing with a book under my arm, went to ball games and read in a book between innings. There being few books in our house, I went book borrowing through the town. The hunger in me found a quick response. Not that we had many intellectuals among us, but there were some, and a few book readers, book lovers. There was the town photographer who loaned me Belamy's *Looking Backward* which sent me off into youthful dreams of a new and beautiful social system in which I might some day live. Other men and women, sensing my passion for books, called me into their houses, "Here, boy. You may read this. Take good care of it. Be sure to bring it back." It was Dickens or Thackeray, and even, now and then, a book of Balzac's.

There were pictures hung on the walls of some of the houses into which I went with boy friends. They were pictures of Emerson, Whittier, Longfellow, Hawthorne. The intellectual life of the northeastern Ohio town was dominated by New England—and there was none of Melville, the greatest of all our pre-Civil War prose men. An odd sort of problem got into my mind. I found a certain dryness, hardness, coldness in the pictured faces. My boy's mind connected them oddly with the town preachers, and we of our family were not churchgoers. Nevertheless these pictured bookwriters were like the preachers—and in me there was this book passion.

I received a key from the superintendent of our town schools, an often violently angry, big-shouldered Irishman with a great black beard. We boys called him Faker Ginn; it was rumored that he went about peeping through keyholes to catch boys throwing spitballs when their teacher's back was turned. An unfair accusation, I am sure. The old style whipping sort of schoolmaster, he had many times tanned my backside. He hated having you make a fuss about it. You were a boy and did certain things. Punishment was necessary. "For God's sake try to take it like a man." Of course, he didn't say quite that.

There was the Irish schoolmaster then who had taken me into his office. This at the end of the school day. I could hear the other kids trooping down a flight of stairs, going into the great outdoors. "Better to get the strapping and have done with it," I would have been thinking. At least if he strapped me, he would not keep me after school.

"You know it's coming to you?"

"Yes sir."

"Then try to take it like a man."

"Yes sir."

He gave it to you vigorously, but if you could take it, it soon stopped.

But the key. There was an occasion when, after such a strapping, at the end of a school day, our schoolmaster took me by the hand.

"Well, that's done. Now you come with me." We went, myself fearfully, through streets to his house, and I remember that it was a brick house on one of our better residence streets. Silently we went along and when we had come to the house, we did not enter by the front door, or by the kitchen door where I had been many times to deliver the family wash, but to a hidden side door that led directly into the schoolmaster's study.

We went in and there the room was. I had never before been in such a room. There were books everywhere. Why, how could there be so many books in all the world? There were shelves of books on all four sides of the room going from the floor to the ceiling. The schoolmaster took a key from a bunch of keys and handed it to me. "It is the key to the outer door to this room." It was the place where he worked, but he was gone all day and often in the evening. I got dimly a sense of something I had never before thought of. In our family, there being seven children, we always living in four- or five-room houses, the rooms in the houses always small, there was not, could not be, such a thing as privacy. . . .

That, compared with the schoolmaster's house— But, dear reader, I am not seeking to ring the changes on the hardships of youth in a house of poverty. . . . I am thinking now entirely of the impression made on a boy's mind by a room, the sense coming to the boy in the room of the schoolmaster.

What? He has a room of his own? He may go into it, sit in here, be undisturbed? The others respect his desire for occasional privacy. Could such a thing ever happen to me? Will I also have a place, a room like this?

"Not surely with so many books. I could never read them all. I could never get at what the writers were trying to say."

There was the schoolmaster standing and looking down at me. I dare say I was barefooted, bare-legged, my feet dirty and dusty. It seems to me now, looking back to that moment, that there was a very beautiful rug on the floor. My imagination had built the little study of the small-town schoolmaster into a kind of palace. Now, in my fancy, the room becomes huge. Once, many years later, I was in the library of the Emperor Napoleon, in his palace at Fontainebleau. Now, in my fancy, the schoolmaster's study seems rather like that.

"There is this key. It is to be yours. I have a duplicate. Except to clean and dust, no one except myself ever comes into this room, and I get little enough time here. There is the door leading to a little side porch. If you come and I am not here it will not upset me.

"The idea is that you may come and go in this room as you please." I must, even at that moment, have known that I would never dare to do it. "You do not behave yourself very well in school, but I do not know that it matters." Could the man have said such a wise thing to me? "It is possible that you may have a mind. There are few enough real minds in the world. I cannot help you much. It may be there are books here that will be of help.

"You are to come and go as you please. You are to take what books you want to read." I am sure the man said nothing about being careful to return the books, nothing of the danger of getting them dirty.

He went about the town, boasting of me.

"He has read more good books than any grown man of this town. He is educating himself thus. He is getting a better education than we could possibly give him in school."

From *Sherwood Anderson's Memoirs*, 1942

Upton Sinclair
1878–1968

HE PULITZER PRIZE-*winning novelist grew up in Baltimore, the son of an alcoholic father and last of an impoverished line of Southern aristocrats. When Sinclair was ten, the family moved to New York City, and four years later he entered City College. He supported himself there, and later at Columbia University Law School, by writing adventure stories for pulp magazines. Although his first novel appeared in 1901, it was with* The Jungle *(1906), his fictional exposé of the Chicago stockyards, that he achieved popular success and notoriety as a "muckraker." Many of his books—over ninety in all—present socialist arguments against big business and capitalism.*

The sordid surroundings in which I was forced to live as a child made me a dreamer. I took to literature, because that was the easiest refuge. I knew practically nothing about music; my mother, with the upbringing of a young lady, could play a few pieces on the piano, but we seldom had a piano, and the music I heard was church hymns, and the plantation melodies that my plump little father hummed while shaving himself with a big razor. My mother had at one time painted pictures; I recall a snow scene in oils, with a kind of tinsel to make sparkles in the snow. But I never learned this wonderful art.

My mother would read books to me, and everything I heard I remembered. I taught myself to read at the age of

Upton Sinclair and son

five, before anyone realized what was happening. I would ask what this letter was, and that, and go away and learn it, and make the sounds, and very soon I was able to take care of myself. I asked my numerous uncles and aunts and cousins to send me only books for Christmas; and now, three quarters of a century later, traces of their gifts are still in my head. Let someone with a taste for research dig into the Christmas books of the early eighties, and find a generous broad volume, with many illustrations, merry rhymes, and a title containing the phrase "a peculiar family." From this book I learned to read, and I would ask my mother if she knew any such "peculiar" persons; for example, the "little boy who was so dreadfully polite, he would not even sneeze unless he asked you if he might." He sneezed by accident, and "scared all the company into the middle of next week."

While arguments between my father and my mother were going on, I was with Gulliver in Lilliput, or on the way to the Celestial City with Christian, or in the shop with the little tailor who killed "seven at one blow." I had Grimm and Andersen and *The Story of the Bible*, and Henty and Alger and Captain Mayne Reid. I would be missing at a party and be discovered behind the sofa with a book. At the home of my Uncle Bland there was an encyclopedia, and my kind uncle was greatly impressed to find me absorbed in the article on gunpowder. Of course, I was pleased to have my zeal for learning admired—but also I really did want to know about gunpowder.

From *The Autobiography of Upton Sinclair*, 1962

H. L. Mencken

H. L. Mencken
1880–1956

HE *"SAGE OF BALTIMORE"*—*otherwise known as Henry Louis Mencken—was born and died in that city by the bay. He has written of "blooding" his first book, and his subsequent discovery of the works of that other American iconoclast, Mark Twain. He went on to become a newspaperman in Baltimore, finding time to co-edit with George Jean Nathan the* Smart Set, *and later the* American Mercury. *Mencken also wrote a body of literary and social criticism that made him one of the most famous and influential figures of the 1920s. His humor and superb writing style have kept his works in print to this day.*

The first long story I ever read was "The Moose Hunters," a tale of the adventures of four half-grown boys in the woods of Maine, published in *Chatterbox* for 1887. *Chatterbox*, which now seems to be pretty well forgotten, was an English annual that had a large sale, in those days, in the American colonies, and "The Moose Hunters" seems to have been printed as a sort of sop or compliment to that trade, just as an English novelist of today lards his narrative with such cheery native bait as "waal, pardner," "you betcha" and "geminy-crickets." The rest of the 1887 issue was made up of intensely English stuff; indeed, it was so English that, reading it and looking at the woodcuts, I sucked in an immense mass of useless information about English history and the English scene, so that to this day I know more about Henry VIII and Lincoln

Cathedral than I know about Millard Fillmore or the Mormon Temple at Salt Lake City.

"The Moose Hunters," which ran to the length of a full-length juvenile, was not printed in one gob, but spread through *Chatterbox* in instalments. This was an excellent device, for literary fans in the youngest brackets do their reading slowly and painfully, and like to come up frequently for air. But writing down to them is something else again, and that error the anonymous author of "The Moose Hunters" avoided diligently. Instead, he wrote in the best journalese of the era, and treated his sixteen-year-old heroes precisely as if they were grown men. So I liked his story very much, and stuck to it until, in a series of perhaps twenty sessions, I had got it down.

This was in the Summer of 1888 and during hot weather, for I remember sitting with the volume on the high marble front steps of our house in Hollins street, in the quiet of approaching dusk, and hearing my mother's warnings that reading by failing light would ruin my eyes. The neighborhood apprentices to gang life went howling up and down the sidewalk, trying to lure me into their games of follow-your-leader and run-sheep-run, but I was not to be lured, for I had discovered a new realm of being and a new and powerful enchantment. What was follow-your-leader to fighting savage Canucks on the Little Magalloway river, and what was chasing imaginary sheep to shooting real meese? I was near the end of the story, with the Canucks all beaten off and two carcasses of gigantic meese hanging to trees, before the author made it clear to me that the word *moose* had no plural, but remained unchanged *ad infinitum*.

Such discoveries give a boy a considerable thrill, and augment his sense of dignity. It is no light matter, at eight, to penetrate suddenly to the difference between *to, two* and *too*, or to that between *run* in baseball and *run* in topographical science, or *cats* and *Katz*. The effect is massive and profound, and at least comparable to that which flows, in later life, out of filling a royal flush or debauching the wife of a major-general of cavalry. I must have made some effort to read *Chatterbox* at the time my Grandmother Mencken gave it to me, which was at Christmas, 1887, but for a while it was no go. I could spell out the shorter pieces at the bottoms of columns, but the longer stories were only jumbles of strange and baffling words. But then, as if by miracle, I found suddenly that I could read them, so I tackled "The Moose Hunters" at once, and stuck to it to the end. There were still, of course, many hard words, but they were no longer insurmountable obstacles. If I staggered and stumbled somewhat, I nevertheless hung on, and by the Fourth of July, 1888, I had blooded my first book.

From *Happy Days: 1880–1892*, 1940

A. A. Milne and his wife

A. A. Milne
1882–1956

LAN ALEXANDER MILNE will forever be associated with his most enduring and endearing creation, Winnie the Pooh. At the age of eleven the London-born author went to Westminster School where he worked diligently for a year, but at twelve "I began to feel that I knew enough and thereafter took life more easily." After completing his studies at Cambridge with "a very moderate degree and a feeling in the family that I had belied the brilliant promise of my youth, and that it was about time I got to work and did something," Milne tried freelance writing for a few years before being saved from penury by obtaining the position of assistant editor at Punch. *After serving in the army during World War I, he wrote a wide variety of works, but it has been the Pooh books that have outlived them all.*

We went to Torquay that summer, and Ken on his fourth birthday was given his first real book *Reynard the Fox*. We both read it. When, forty years later, I wrote a book called *Winnie-the-Pooh* and saw Shepard's drawing of Pooh, the bear, standing on the branch of a tree outside Owl's house, I remembered all that *Reynard the Fox* and *Uncle Remus* and the animal stories in *Aunt Judy's Magazine* had meant to us. Even if none of their magic had descended on me, at least it had inspired my collaborator; and I had the happy feeling that here was a magic which children, from generation to generation, have been unable to resist. *Uncle Remus* was read aloud to us by Papa, a chapter a night. One night he had to go away. Little knowing what we were doing we handed the sacred book to our governess, and told her to go on from there. Some such experience, no doubt, caused the first man to coin the phrase that he "could not believe his ears." Terrible things were happening all around us. Was this Uncle Remus? Was this our own beloved Bee? One of our idols had to go. Stumbling painfully through the dialect, Bee got to the bottom of the page and asked if she should go on. We said not. It wasn't very interesting, she thought. We thought not too. Should she read another book, or should we play a game? We played a game. Next night we found the place for Papa. Three lines in that lovely understanding voice, and Uncle Remus was saved. But Bee never read aloud again. She was a darling; I still loved her; but I was glad that I was marrying Molly.

From *Autobiography*, 1939

Will Durant
1885–1981

N 1935 WILL DURANT *gave up his position as a philosophy professor to become a full-time writer, and completed the first book of what would become the eleven volume* Story of Civilization. *Over the next forty years Durant and his wife Ariel continued work on their popularized history, earning a Pulitzer Prize for their efforts. Born in North Adams, Massachusetts, Durant moved with his family to a small New Jersey town while he was still a child. In one of his memoirs he remembers a young girl named Irene, his first love, and his introduction to literature.*

. . . One day I saw in Irene's hand a book called *Pickwick Papers*. I opened it and was at once allured by the abundance of conversation it contained; here was a lively book and a juicy one and it was so immense—seven or eight hundred pages; surely the author had been paid by the page, and had had an extravagant wife. I thought it would be quite a feat to read such a volume through; perhaps I should be the first boy in the world to accomplish it. But what moved me most was that it was Irene's book; it must be good if her soft hands had touched it and her bright eyes had traveled along its lines. I begged it from her, and that night, against the protest of my parents, I burned the midnight oil over the adventures of the Pickwick Club, and Sam Weller, and the fat boy who always fell asleep. O happy and undisillusioned Victorians! maligned and misunderstood, what a delight it must have

Will and Ariel Durant

been to watch the creation, week after week, of that incomparable imaginary world! What a delight it was even now, across a thousand obscuring differences of land and speech and time, to know this vivacious style, this inexhaustible drama, this endless chain of existing incident! I read every word and marvelled that I had lived twelve years without discovering the book. I returned it to Irene, and begged her for more.

"It's all I have by Dickens," she said, sorrowfully. "But Papa says he'll get me *David Copperfield* for Christmas."

Christmas was several months away; I could not wait that long. Within a week I had managed to accumulate fourteen pennies; and armed with them I walked the three miles between our new home in Arlington and Dressel's book-store in Newark. I asked the grouchy old gentleman behind the counter for the cheapest edition of *David Copperfield*. He went into a rear room, worked his way precariously among stacks of brokendown books, and emerged with a copy that might have rivaled Ulysses' wanderings.

"I will let this go for twenty five cents," he said, munificently.

My heart was broke temporarily.

"But mister," I said, with a politeness which I seldom achieved, "I've only got fourteen cents."

He was unmoved, and turned away to another customer. I looked longingly at the book, and helplessly at space in general. Then a tall handsome gentleman, whom I conceived as a millionaire philosopher but who turned out to be a butcher, came over to me and put his arm around my shoulder.

"What do you want, sonny?" he said.

"*David Copperfield*," I replied.

"How much do you need?"

"Eleven cents."

"Is that all? Here you are; when you get rich you can pay me back."

Fortunately, he is dead now. But I was so grateful that I could not speak. I accepted the eleven cents as a gift from God, and walked out of the store in a daze. I trudged home in ecstasy over the kindness of Providence, the goodness of human nature, and the pleasures in store for me in the 860 pages which I carried under my arm.

From that day I became a tremendous reader. When everybody else in the house was asleep I would read on, despite a thousand admonitions about the injury I was doing to my health, and the cost of gas. It is true that I lost something of my taste for sport, and more of my skill in it. I could not play with "Dots" Miller, or "shoot" marbles with Jimmy Calmar any more. But what a new universe I had found! I no longer lived in prosaic New Jersey; I wandered around the world with my heroes and my poets. . . .

From *Transition: A Sentimental Story of One Mind and One Era*, 1927

e. e. cummings
1894–1962

 OUNG EDWARD ESTLIN CUMMINGS spent his childhood in Cambridge, Massachusetts. After attending Harvard, he went to France in 1917 as a volunteer ambulance driver, remaining there after the war to study art and write. Upon his return, he took up residence in New York's Greenwich Village and devoted himself to writing poetry. Often recognized for his eccentric yet powerful use of form and punctuation, Cummings proclaimed in the introduction to his Collected Poems *that his work was "for you and for me and not for most people."*

After myself and my father and mother, I loved most dearly my mother's brother George. He was by profession a lawyer, by inclination a bon vivant, and by nature a joyous human being. When this joyous human being wasn't toiling in his office, or hobnobbing with so-called swells at the Brookline country club, he always became my playfellow. No more innocently good-hearted soul ever kissed the world good-night; but when it came to literature, bloodthirsty was nothing to him. And (speaking of bloodthirstiness) I here devoutly thank a beneficent Providence for allowing me to live my childhood and my boyhood and even my youth without ever glimpsing that typical item of an era of at least penultimate confusion—the uncomic nonbook. No paltry supermen, no shadowy space-cadets, no trifling hyperjunglequeens and pantless pantherwomen insulted my virginal imagination. I read or was read, at an early age, the most immemorial

e. e. cummings, self portrait

myths, the wildest wild animal stories, lots of Scott and
quantities of Dickens (including the immortal *Pickwick Papers*), *Robinson Crusoe* and *The Swiss Family Robinson*, *Gulliver's Travels*, *Twenty Thousand Leagues Under the Sea*, poetry
galore, The Holy Bible, and *The Arabian Nights*. One city
winter I floated through chivalry with Mallory and Froissart:
the following country summer—we had by then acquired
a farm—I dressed as a Red Indian, slept in a teepee, and
almost punctured our best Jersey cow with a random arrow;
in emulation of the rightful inhabitants of my wrongful native land.

A gruesome history of the Tower of London had been
conscientiously compiled by a prominent British prelate, en-
dowed with what would now be termed sadistic trends; and
suddenly this feaful opus burgeoned in our midst. Every
night after dinner, if George were on deck, he would rub his
hands and wink magnificently in my direction and call to my
maiden aunt "Jane, let's have some ruddy gore!" whereupon
Jane would protestingly join us in the parlour; and George
would stealthily produce the opus; and she would blushfully
read; and I would cling to the sofa in exquisite terror.
We also read—for sheer relaxation—*Lorna Doone* (with
whom I fell sublimely in love) and *Treasure Island* (as a result
of which, the blind pirate Pew followed me upstairs for
weeks; while for months, if not years, one-legged John Silver
stood just behind me as my trembling fingers fumbled the
electric light chain).

From *i: six nonlectures*, 1953

Jean Rhys

Jean Rhys
1894–1979

 EAN RHYS *was born and raised in the Windward Islands of the Caribbean, the daughter of a Welsh physician and a native-born mother. At sixteen, she came to England where she held a number of jobs—chorus girl, mannequin, artist's model—and only began to write after moving to Paris when the first of her three marriages broke up. After the first publication of her novels in the 1920s and 1930s Rhys lapsed into obscurity for twenty-seven years until her sudden reappearance in 1966 with the publication of* Wide Sargasso Sea, *for which she won the Royal Society of Literature Award as well as long-deserved recognition for her entire* oeuvre.

Before I could read, almost a baby, I imagined that God, this strange thing or person I heard about, was a book. Sometimes it was a large book standing upright and half open and I could see the print inside but it made no sense to me. Other times the book was smaller and inside were sharp flashing things. The smaller book was, I am sure now, my mother's needle book, and the sharp flashing things were her needles with the sun on them.

I was so slow learning to read that my parents had become worried about me. Then suddenly, with a leap as it were, I could manage quite long words. Soon I could make sense of the fairy stories Irish Granny sent—the red, the blue, the green, the yellow. Then she sent *The Heroes, The Adventures of Ulysses, Perseus and Andromeda.* I read everything I could get hold of. There was the usual glassed-in bookcase at the end of the sitting room, but it was never locked, the key was lost, and the only warning was that we must keep it shut, for the books must be protected against insects.

I can still see the volumes of the *Encyclopaedia Britannica* that I never touched, a large bible and several history books, yellow-backed novels and on the top shelf a rather odd selection of poets, Milton, Byron, then Crabbe, Cowper, Mrs. Hemans, also *Robinson Crusoe*, *Treasure Island*, *Gulliver's Travels*, *Pilgrim's Progress*.

My nurse, who was called Meta, didn't like me much anyway, and complete with a book it was too much. One day she found me crouched on the staircase reading a bowdlerized version of *The Arabian Nights* in very small print.

She said, "If all you read so much, you know what will happen to you? Your eyes will drop out and they will look at you from the page."

"If my eyes dropped out I wouldn't see," I argued.

She said, "They drop out except the little black points you see with."

I half believed her and imagined my pupils like heads of black pins and all the rest gone. But I went on reading.

From *Smile Please: An Unfinished Autobiography*, 1979

C. S. Lewis
1898–1963

LIVE STAPLES LEWIS was the author of an impressive array of books, both popular and scholarly in nature, including The Screwtape Letters *(1942) and the* Chronicles of Narnia *series (1950–1956). Until shortly before his death he held the Chair of Medieval and Renaissance English Literature at Cambridge. Born at Belfast in Northern Ireland, he was the son of a solicitor and of a clergyman's daughter, both of whom were of a bookish nature. However, neither had the least taste for the kind of literature which Lewis loved. They never listened, he wrote, "for the horns of elfland. There was no copy either of Keats or Shelley in the house, and the copy of Coleridge was never (to my knowledge) opened." When he was seven, the family moved to a larger home. The "New House," as they continued to call it, was so large that it seemed to the child less like a house than a city.*

. . . To me, the important thing about the move was that the background of my life became larger. The New House is almost a major character in my story. I am a product of long corridors, empty sunlit rooms, upstairs indoor silences, attics explored in solitude, distant noises of gurgling cisterns and pipes, and the noise of wind under the tiles. Also, of endless books. My father bought all the books he read and never got rid of any of them. There were books in the study, books in the drawing room, books in the cloakroom, books

C. S. Lewis

(two deep) in the great bookcase on the landing, books in a bedroom, books piled as high as my shoulder in the cistern attic, books of all kinds reflecting every transient stage of my parents' interest, books readable and unreadable, books suitable for a child and books most emphatically not. Nothing was forbidden me. In the seemingly endless rainy afternoons I took volume after volume from the shelves. I had always the same certainty of finding a book that was new to me as a man who walks into a field has of finding a new blade of grass. Where all these books had been before we came to the New House is a problem that never occurred to me until I began writing this paragraph. I have no idea of the answer. . . . Of the books that I read at this time very few have quite faded from memory, but not all have retained my love. Conan Doyle's *Sir Nigel*, which first set my mind upon "knights in armor," I have never felt inclined to reread. Still less would I now read Mark Twain's *A Connecticut Yankee in King Arthur's Court*, which was then my only source for the Arthurian story, blissfully read for the sake of the romantic elements that came through and with total disregard of the vulgar ridicule directed against them. Much better than either of these was E. Nesbit's trilogy, *Five Children and It*, *The Phoenix and the Wishing Carpet*, and *The Amulet*. The last did most for me. It first opened my eyes to antiquity, the "dark backward and abysm of time." I can still reread it with delight. *Gulliver* in an unexpurgated and lavishly illustrated edition was one of my favorites, and I pored endlessly over an almost complete set of old *Punches* which stood in my father's study. Tenniel gratified my passion for "dressed animals" with his Russian Bear, British Lion, Egyptian Crocodile and the rest, while his slovenly and perfunctory treatment of vegetation confirmed my own deficiencies. Then came the Beatrix Potter books, and here at last beauty.

From *Surprised by Joy: The Shape of My Early Life*, 1954

John Steinbeck with his third wife, Elaine Scott

John Steinbeck
1902–1968

HE SALINAS VALLEY *in California where the*
Nobel Prize-winning novelist was born—and
the neighboring Monterey coast—is a region
that Steinbeck would make peculiarly his own
in such novels as Tortilla Flats, Cannery Row, *and* East
of Eden. *Before beginning his career as a writer, he studied*
marine biology at Stanford, and later worked at a variety of
jobs, including fruit picking—an experience which would later
prove useful in documenting the plight of the Joad family
in his Pulitzer Prize-winning novel
The Grapes of Wrath.

Some people there are who, being grown, forget the horrible
task of learning to read. It is perhaps the greatest single effort
that the human undertakes, and he must do it as a child. An
adult is rarely successful in the undertaking—the reduction
of experience to a set of symbols. For a thousand thousand
years these humans have existed and they have only learned
this trick—this magic—in the final ten thousand of the thousand thousand.

I do not know how usual my experience is, but I have seen
in my children the appalled agony of trying to learn to read.
They, at least, have my experience.

I remember that words—written or printed—were devils,
and books, because they gave me pain, were my enemies.

Some literature was in the air around me. The Bible I
absorbed through my skin. My uncles exuded Shakespeare,

and *Pilgrim's Progress* was mixed with my mother's milk. But these things came into my ears. They were sounds, rhythms, figures. Books were printed demons—the tongs and thumb-screws of outrageous persecution. And then, one day, an aunt gave me a book and fatuously ignored my resentment. I started at the black print with hatred, and then, gradually, the pages opened and let me in. The magic happened. The Bible and Shakespeare and *Pilgrim's Progress* belonged to everyone. But this was mine— It was a cut version of the Caxton *Morte d'Arthur* of Thomas Malory. I loved the old spelling of the words—and the words no longer used. Perhaps a passionate love for the English language opened to me from this one book. I was delighted to find out paradoxes— that *cleave* means both to stick together and to cut apart; that *host* means both an enemy and a welcoming friend; that *king* and *gens* (people) stem from the same root. For a long time, I had a secret language—*yclept* and *hyght*, *wist*—and *accord* meaning peace, and *entente* meaning purpose, and *fyaunce* meaning promise. Moving my lips, I pronounced the letter known as *thorn*, þ, like a "p," which it resembles, instead of like a "th." But in my town, the first word of Ye Olde Pye Shoppe was pronounced "yee," so I guess my betters were no better off than I. It was much later that I discovered that "y" had been substituted for the lost þ. But beyond the glorious and secret words—" And when the chylde is borne lete it be delyvered to me at yonder privy posterne uncrys-tened"—oddly enough I knew the words from whispering them to myself. The very strangeness of the language dyd me enchante, and vaulted me into an ancient scene.

And in that scene were all the vices that ever were—and courage and sadness and frustration, but particularly gal-lantry—perhaps the only single quality of man that the West has invented. I think my sense of right and wrong, my feeling of noblesse oblige, and any thought I may have against the oppressor and for the oppressed, came from this secret book. It did not outrage my sensibilities as nearly all the children's books did. It did not seem strange to me that Uther Pendragon wanted the wife of his vassal and took her by trickery. I was not frightened to find that there were evil knights, as well as noble ones. In my own town there were men who wore the clothes of virtue whom I knew to be bad. In pain or sorrow or confusion, I went back to my magic book. Children are violent and cruel—and good—and I was all of these—and all of these were in the secret book. If I could not choose my way at the crossroads of love and loyalty, neither could Lancelot. I could understand the darkness of Mordred because he was in me too; and there was some Galahad in me, but perhaps not enough. The Grail feeling was there, however, deep-planted, and perhaps always will be.

From *The Acts of King Arthur and His Noble Knights: From the Winchester Manuscripts of Thomas Malory and Other Sources*, 1976

Isaac Bashevis Singer

Isaac Bashevis Singer
1904–

*T*HOSE WHO ARE *familiar with the Nobel-Prize-winning author's autobiographical volumes know that he was born in Radzymin, Poland, into a family where "religion, Jewishness, was virtually the air that we breathed," and that he emigrated to the United States in 1935, settling in New York City. There he began to write in Yiddish for the* Jewish Daily Forward, *where over the ensuing decades he published his stories. The offspring of generations of rabbis, Singer sought the answers to his questions about the nature of existence early in life—truly, as the title of one of his memoirs puts it, "a little boy in search of God." Wanting to get hold of books by the secular philosophers, but not knowing where to find them, he stumbled upon an overdue book of his brother's from Besler's Library on Nowolipki Street.*

. . . Now I was ready to launch the biggest adventure of my life—namely, I resolved to go to this library and try to get a book out on philosophy. It was my feeling that my brother had probably already read this book and that it was high time he brought it back. A few times cards had come from the library demanding from my brother that he bring back books that were overdue. I would therefore take this book back and ask for another in his stead, one on philosophy. It was true that if my brother found out what I had done, he might grow terribly angry and might even slap me for going where I didn't belong. But what was a slap compared to the joy that a book on philosophy would grant me? I burned with the urge to read what the philosophers had to say about God, the world, time, space, and, most of all, why people and animals suffer so. This to me was the question of questions.

I took the book and started off toward Nowolipki Street. It was freezing outside. The Germans had pushed so close to Warsaw that I could hear their cannonfire in the streets. I pictured to myself how a thousand soldiers died from every shot. Freezing blasts blew, making my nose feel like a piece of wood. I had no gloves, and the fingers of the hand holding the book had become stiff. I was terribly afraid they would yell at me at the library or make fun of me. Who knows? My brother might even be there. I raced against the wind, and a voice within me shouted, "I must learn the truth! Once and for all!"

I went inside the library and, for a moment, saw nothing. My eyes grew bedazzled and my head spun. "If only I don't faint!" I prayed to the forces that guided the world. Gradually the dizziness subsided, and I saw a huge room, actually a hall stacked with books from floor to the astoundingly high ceiling. The sun shone in through the windows casting a bright wintery light. Behind a wide counter stood a corpulent man—bareheaded, beardless, with longish hair and a mustache—who placed paper patches on the margins of a book. For a long time he didn't look up, then he noticed me, and his big black eyes expressed a kind of amiable surprise.

He said: "What do you say, young fellow?"

I savored the title "young fellow." It was a sign that I was already half grown.

I replied: "I brought back my brother's book."

The librarian stuck out his hand and took the book. He stared for a long time at the inside of the cover and knitted his brow. Then he asked: "Israel Joshua Singer is your brother?"

"Yes, my older brother," I replied.

"What's happened to him? It's a year since he took out this book. You're not allowed to keep a book longer than a month. A pretty big fine has accumulated. More than the deposit."

"My brother is in the Army," I said, astounded over my own lie. It was obviously either my way of justifying my brother's failure to return the book or a means of drawing sympathy to myself. The librarian shook his head.

"Where is he—in the war?"

"Yes, the war."

"You don't hear from him?"

"Not a word."

The librarian grimaced.

"What do they want—those savages? Why do they drag innocent victims into their murderous wars?" He spoke half to me, half to himself. He paused a moment, then said: "Your brother is a talented man. He writes well. He paints well, too. A talent. A born talent. Well, and you obviously study at the study house, eh?"

"Yes, I study, but I want to know what goes on in the world, too," I said. I had the feeling that my mouth was speaking of its own volition.

"Oh? What do you want to know?"

"Oh—physics, geography, philosophy—everything."

"Everything, eh? No one knows everything."

"I want to know the secret of life," I said, ashamed of my own words. "I want to read a book on philosophy."

The librarian arched his brows.

"What book? In what language?"

"In Yiddish. I understand Hebrew, too."

"You mean, the sacred language?"

"My brother read the *Ha-tzephirah*, and I read it, too."

"And your father let you read such a heretical paper?"

"He didn't see."

The librarian mulled this over.

"I have something about philosophy in Yiddish, but a boy your age should study useful things, not philosophy. It'll be difficult for you and it'll serve no practical purpose."

"I want to know what the philosophers say about why people must suffer and how the world came about."

"The philosophers don't know this themselves. Wait here."

He went to search among the books and even climbed a ladder. He came down with two books and showed them to me. One was in Yiddish, the other in Hebrew.

He said: "I have something for you, but if your father should see them, he'd tear them to pieces."

"My father won't see them. I'll hide them well."

"When you take out books from a library, you have to leave a deposit and pay for a month in advance, but you probably haven't a *groschen*. All right, I'll take the chance, but bring them back when you're finished. And keep them clean. If you bring them back in time, I'll find something else for you. If a boy wants to learn the secret of life, you have to accommodate him."

The librarian smiled and marked something down on cards. He handed me the books, and I barely restrained myself from kissing his hand. A great surge of affection swept over me toward this good person along with the desperate urge to read what was written in these books.

From *A Little Boy in Search of God: Mysticism in a Personal Light*, 1976

Richard Wright
1908–1960

HE AUTHOR *of* Native Son *(1940) left his home in Mississippi for Memphis, Tennessee, at the age of seventeen. With the small amount of money he earned as an errand boy, be began buying secondhand magazines and books for a few cents, reading them, then reselling them. One morning he saw a newspaper article furiously denouncing H. L. Mencken. "I wondered what on earth this Mencken could have done to call down upon him the scorn of the South." Wanting to find out about Mencken, he knew of the huge library near the river front, but also knew that blacks were not allowed to use it. Finally, he screwed up enough courage to ask a white man on the job if he would let him use his library card. Wright then wrote a note to the library over that man's signature to the effect that he was sending the "boy" to pick up books for him: "Dear Madam: Will you please let this nigger boy have some books by H. L. Mencken?" The book that he received changed his life, becoming a "literary bible" for him for years.*

That night in my rented room, while letting the hot water run over my can of pork and beans in the sink, I opened *A Book of Prefaces* and began to read. I was jarred and shocked by the style, the clear, clean, sweeping sentences. Why did he write like that? And how did one write like that? I pictured the man as a raging demon, slashing with his pen, consumed

Richard Wright (left) with Gaston Monnerville (right)
and George Slocombe (center)

with hate, denouncing everything American, extolling everything European or German, laughing at the weaknesses of
people, mocking God, authority. What was this? I stood up,
trying to realize what reality lay behind the meaning of the
words . . . Yes, this man was fighting, fighting with words.
He was using words as a weapon, using them as one would
use a club. Could words be weapons? Well, yes, for here
they were. Then, maybe, perhaps, I could use them as a
weapon? No. It frightened me. I read on and what amazed
me was not what he said, but how on earth anybody had the
courage to say it. . . . I concluded the book with the convic-
tion that I had somehow overlooked something terribly important in life. I had once tried to write, had once reveled in
feeling, had let my crude imagination roam, but the impulse
to dream had been slowly beaten out of me by experience.
Now it surged up again and I hungered for books, new ways
of looking and seeing. It was not a matter of believing or
disbelieving what I read, but of feeling something new, of
being affected by something that made the look of the world
different.

As dawn broke I ate my pork and beans, feeling dopey,
sleepy. I went to work, but the mood of the book would not
die; it lingered, coloring everything I saw, heard, did. I now
felt that I knew what the white men were feeling. Merely
because I had read a book that had spoken of how they lived
and thought, I identified myself with that book. I felt vaguely
guilty. Would I, filled with bookish notions, act in a manner
that would make the whites dislike me?

I forged more notes and my trips to the library became
frequent. Reading grew into a passion. . . . The plots and
stories in the novels did not interest me so much as the point
of view revealed. I gave myself over to each novel without
reserve, without trying to criticize it; it was enough for me
to see and feel something different. And for me, everything

was something different. Reading was like a drug, a dope. The novels created moods in which I lived for days. But I could not conquer my sense of guilt, my feeling that the white men around me knew that I was changing, that I had begun to regard them differently.

Whenever I brought a book to the job, I wrapped it in newspaper—a habit that was to persist for years in other cities and under other circumstances. But some of the white men pried into my packages when I was absent and they questioned me.

"Boy, what are you reading those books for?"

"Oh, I don't know, sir."

"That's deep stuff you're reading, boy."

"I'm just killing time, sir."

"You'll addle your brains if you don't watch out."

I read Dreiser's *Jennie Gerhardt* and *Sister Carrie* and they revived in me a vivid sense of my mother's suffering; I was overwhelmed. I grew silent, wondering about the life around me. It would have been impossible for me to have told anyone what I derived from these novels, for it was nothing less than a sense of life itself. All my life had shaped me for the realism, the naturalism of the modern novel, and I could not read enough of them.

. . . In buoying me up, reading also cast me down, made me see what was possible, what I had missed. My tension returned, new, terrible, bitter, surging, almost too great to be contained. I no longer *felt* that the world about me was hostile, killing; I *knew* it. A million times I asked myself what I could do to save myself, and there were no answers. I seemed forever condemned, ringed by walls.

. . . I knew of no Negroes who read the books I liked and I wondered if any Negroes ever thought of them. I knew that there were Negro doctors, lawyers, newspapermen, but I never saw any of them. When I read a Negro newspaper I

never caught the faintest echo of my preoccupation in its
pages. I felt trapped and occasionally, for a few days, I would
stop reading. But a vague hunger would come over me for
books, books that opened up new avenues of feeling and
seeing, and again I would forge another note to the white
librarian. Again I would read and wonder as only the naïve
and unlettered can read and wonder, feeling that I carried a
secret, criminal burden about with me each day.

From *Black Boy: A Record of Childhood and Youth*, 1945

M. F. K. Fisher

M. F. K. Fisher
1908–

LTHOUGH MARY FRANCES *Kennedy Fisher was born in Albion, Michigan, she spent her childhood in Whittier, California, where her father was the publisher of the local newspaper. Since the appearance of* Serve It Forth *in 1937, Fisher has become renowned for her gastronomical writings. She has also written novels, short stories, poetry, travel books, an autobiography and a sceenplay, and did an acclaimed translation of Brillat-Savarin's classic* The Physiology of Taste. *Over the years she has come to be recognized as one of the finest American writers of her time; in fact, W. H. Auden once wrote that he "did not know of anyone in the U.S. today who writes better prose."*

I cannot remember how I learned to read. I am sure nobody said, "Now we are going to . . ." and then proceeded to show me the trick. Everybody in the house who could follow a printed sentence read aloud. Grandmother read the Bible to me. Mother read whatever she was reading, if I was within earshot . . . the Los Angeles *Times*, an old copy of *Punch*, a page from whatever novel she was into. Father read headlines at the breakfast table. In the kitchen Mother would read a recipe to the cook and try to explain it and then I would, from memory, show the cook the words again. And of course there were always the books Grandmother bought, with a big eye meaning "I."

I did stay out of school until I was seven, of course, but

by the time I was going on five I had reading in my own hands. I started to practice, apparently, on one of the Oz books, and whether it was because the story was pagan fantasy or not, my grandmother asked Rex to send me to the Spare Room, because I seemed to have to read in a high slow keening shriek.

This was a special treat for me, since Anne and I were not allowed in the cold ugly room (dark green with mahogany), unless Mother was ill or something like that. Usually it was occupied by various Holbrook kith and kin.

I lay voluptuously on my stomach on the big bed, blissfully alone, and I felt a thrill which has never left me as I realized that the words coming magically from my lips were mine to say or not say, read or not. It was one of the peaks of my whole life. Slowly my eyes rode across the lines of print, and the New World smiled. It was mine, not something to beg for, book in hand, from anyone who could read when I could not. The door opened, and without hesitation I walked through.

I feel quite sure that this first book was *The Wizard of Oz*, because there was some cynicism on Grandmother's part when I announced that I had finished it upstairs. She sniffed, and rightly, that I already knew it by heart from hearing my mother, and was simply repeating the words. To prove her wrong I did what now seems to me an odd thing, and I removed somehow from her sacrosanct apartment (the third addition my parents made to the new house, a large bed-sitting room and bath and dressing room off the living room, with a softly sliding door which we never opened uninvited) a tiny book called *The Imitation of Christ*. Its soft black leather binding and its size had long tantalized me, when I went into Grandmother's room to fetch her glasses or handkerchief, and apparently I palmed it quite easily. I scanned it aloud, upstairs, and then went right to Mother, to show her that I could indeed read something I had never known before, no matter what it might be. To my surprise she laughed helplessly through several pages of my innocent inflectings of Thomas a Kempis' far from frivolous suggestions for a contemplative life. When she could stand no more, she embraced me strongly, and then took the darling little book to replace, the next time she was near her mother's desk.

She told me she was very proud that I could read, and suggested that I ask Grandmother, after supper, if she would like me to try a bit of the Old Testament aloud. That should prove my point. And so, apparently, I did, for after that I often read the Bible as Grandmother knitted hideous khaki-colored socks and mittens for the Poor Tommies and then for Our Boys. She would not stand for any singsong or carelessness, very good for me, and when she asked me sharply what I thought a new word meant, and I had no answer, I was sent straight to the dictionary, which I learned to use long before I started school.

From *Among Friends*, 1971

Eudora Welty

Eudora Welty

1909–

ROWING UP *in Jackson, Mississippi, Eudora
Welty was introduced to the way of words at an
early age. She has written in her memoir,* One
Writer's Beginnings *(1984):*

> *I live in gratitude to my parents for initiating me—
> and as early as I begged for it, without keeping me
> waiting—into knowledge of the word, into reading
> and spelling, by way of the alphabet. They taught me
> to begin reading before starting to school . . .*

*She began to write as well as read and since the publication
of her first collection of short stories she has been deemed one
of America's most distinguished writers, recipient both of the
Pulitzer Prize and the prestigious Howells Medal conferred
by the American Academy and Institute of
Arts and Letters.*

When I used to ask my mother which we were, rich or poor,
she refused to tell me. I was then nine years old and of course
what I was dying to hear was that we were poor. I was
reading a book called *Five Little Peppers* and my heart was
set on baking a cake for my mother in a stove with a hole in
it. Some version of rich, crusty old Mr. King—up till that
time not living on our street—was sure to come down the
hill in his wheelchair and rescue me if anything went wrong.
But before I could start a cake at all I had to find out if we
were poor, and poor *enough*; and my mother wouldn't tell

me, she said she was too busy. I couldn't wait too long;
I had to go on reading and soon Polly Pepper got into
more trouble, some that was a little harder on her and easier
on me.

Trouble, the backbone of literature, was still to me the
original property of the fairy tale, and as long as there was
plenty of trouble for everybody and the rewards for it were
falling in the right spots, reading was all smooth sailing. At
that age a child reads with higher appetite and gratification,
and with those two stars sailing closer together, than ever
again in his growing up. The home shelves had been provid-
ing me all along with the usual books, and I read them with
love—but snap, I finished them. I read everything just alike—
snap. I even came to the *Tales from Maria Edgeworth* and went
right ahead, without feeling the bump—then. It *was* notice-
able that when her characters suffered she punished them for
it, instead of rewarding them as a reader had rather been led
to hope. In her stories, the children had to make their choice
between being unhappy and good about it and being unhappy
and bad about it, and then she helped them to choose wrong.
In *The Purple Jar*, it will be remembered, there was the little
girl being taken through the shops by her mother and her
downfall coming when she chooses to buy something beautiful instead of something necessary. The purple jar, when
the shop sends it out, proves to have been purple only so
long as it was filled with purple water, and her mother knew
it all the time. They don't deliver the water. That's only the
cue for stones to start coming through the hole in the victim's
worn-out shoe. She bravely agrees she must keep walking
on stones until such time as she is offered another choice
between the beautiful and the useful. Her father tells her as
far as he is concerned she can stay in the house. If I had been
at all easy to disappoint, that story would have disappointed
me. Of course I did feel what is the good of walking on

rocks if they are going to let the water out of the jar too? And it seemed to me that even the illustrator fell down on the characters in that book, not alone Maria Edgeworth, for when a rich, crusty old gentleman gave Simple Susan a guinea for some kind deed she'd done him, there was a picture of the transaction and where was the guinea? I couldn't make out a feather. But I liked *reading* the book all right—except that I finished it.

My mother took me to the Public Library and introduced me: "Let her have any book she wants, except *Elsie Dinsmore*." I looked for the book I couldn't have and it was a row. That was how I learned about the Series Books. The *Five Little Peppers* belonged, so did *The Wizard of Oz*, so did *The Little Colonel*, so did *The Green Fairy Book*. There were many of everything, generations of everybody, instead of one. I wasn't coming to the end of reading, after all—I was saved.

Our library in those days was a big rotunda lined with shelves. A copy of *V. V.'s Eyes* seemed to follow you wherever you went, even after you'd read it. I didn't know what I liked, I just knew what there was a lot of. After *Randy's Spring* there came *Randy's Summer*, *Randy's Fall* and *Randy's Winter*. True, I didn't care very much myself for her spring, but it didn't occur to me that I might not care for her summer, and then her summer didn't prejudice me against her fall, and I still had hopes as I moved on to her winter. I was disappointed in her whole year as it turned out, but a thing like that didn't keep me from wanting to read every word of it. The pleasures of reading itself—who doesn't remember?— were like those of a Christmas cake, a sweet devouring. The "Randy Books" failed chiefly in being so soon over. Four seasons doesn't make a series.

All that summer I used to put on a second petticoat (our librarian wouldn't let you past the front door if she could see through you), ride my bicycle up the hill and "through the Capitol" (short cut) to the library with my two read books in the basket (two was the limit you could take out at one time when you were a child and also as long as you lived), and tiptoe in ("Silence") and exchange them for two more in two minutes. Selection was no object. I coasted the two new books home, jumped out of my petticoat, read (I suppose I ate and bathed and answered questions put to me), then in all hope put my petticoat back on and rode those two books back to the library to get my next two.

The librarian was the lady in town who wanted to be it. She called me by my full name and said: "Does your mother know where you are? You know good and well the fixed rule of this library: *Nobody is going to come running back here with any book on the same day they took it out.* Get both those things out of here and don't come back till tomorrow. And I can practically see through you."

My great-aunt in Virginia, who understood better about needing more to read than you *could* read, sent me a book so big it had to be read on the floor—a bound volume of six or eight issues of *St. Nicholas* from a previous year. In the very first pages a serial began: *The Lucky Stone* by Abbie Farwell Brown. The illustrations were right down my alley: a heroine so poor she was ragged, a witch with an extremely pointed hat, a rich, crusty old gentleman in—better than a wheelchair—a runaway carriage; and I set to. I gobbled up installment after installment through the whole luxurious book, through the last one, and then came the words, turning me to *un*lucky stone: "To be concluded." The book had come to an end and The Lucky Stone wasn't finished! The witch had it! I couldn't believe this infidelity from my aunt. I still had my secret childhood feeling that if you hunted long enough in a book's pages you could find what you were looking for, and long after I knew books better than that I used to hunt again for the end of *The Lucky Stone*. It never occurred to me that the story had an existence anywhere else outside the pages of that single green-bound book. The last chapter was just something I would have to do without. Polly Pepper could do it. And then suddenly I tried something—I read it again, as much as I had of it. I was in love with books at least partly for what they looked like; I loved the printed page.

In my little circle books were almost never given for Christmas, they cost too much. But the year before I'd been given a book and got a shock. It was from the same classmate who had told me there was no Santa Claus. She gave me a book, all right—*Poems by Another Little Girl*. It looked like a real book, was printed like a real book—but it was *by her*. *Homemade* poems? Illusion-dispelling was her favorite game. She was in such a hurry, she had such a pile to get rid of— her mother's electric runabout was stacked to the bud vases with copies—that she hadn't even time to say, "Merry Christmas!" With only the same raucous laugh with which she had told me, "Been filling my own stocking for years!" she shot me her book, received my Japanese pencil box with a moonlight scene on the lid and a sharpened pencil inside, jumped back into the car and was sped away by her mother. I stood right where they had left me, on the curb in my Little Nurse's uniform, and read that book, and I had no better way to prove when I got through than I had when I started that this was not a real book. But of course it wasn't. The printed page is not absolutely everything.

Then this Christmas was coming, and my grandfather in Ohio sent along in his box of presents an envelope with money in it for me to buy myself the book I wanted.

I went to Kress's. Not everybody knew Kress's sold books, but children just before Christmas know everything Kress's ever sold or will sell. My father had showed us the mirror he was giving my mother to hang above her desk, and Kress's is where my brother and I went to reproduce that by buying a mirror together to give her ourselves, and where our little brother then made us take him and he bought her one his size for fifteen cents. Kress's had also its version of the Series Book, called, exactly like another series, "The Camp Fire Girls," beginning with *The Camp Fire Girls in the Woods*.

I believe they were ten cents each and I had a dollar. But they weren't all that easy to buy, because the series stuck, and to buy some of it was like breaking into a loaf of French bread. Then after you got home, each single book was as hard to open as a box stuck in its varnish, and when it gave way it popped like a firecracker. The covers once prized apart would never close; those books once open stayed open and lay on their backs helplessly fluttering their leaves like a turned-over June bug. They were as light as a matchbox. They were printed on yellowed paper with corners that crumbled, if you pinched on them too hard, like old graham crackers, and they smelled like attic trunks, caramelized glue, their own confinement with one another and, over all, the Kress's smell—bandanas, peanuts and sandalwood from the incense counter. Even without reading them I loved them. It was hard, that year, that Christmas is a day you can't read.

What could have happened to those books?—but I can tell you about the leading character. His name was Mr. Holmes. He was not a Camp Fire Girl: he wanted to catch one. Through every book of the series he gave chase. He pursued Bessie and Zara—those were the Camp Fire Girls—and kept scooping them up in his touring car, while they just as regularly got away from him. Once Bessie escaped from the second floor of a strange inn by climbing down a gutter pipe. Once she escaped by driving away from Mr. Holmes in his own automobile, which she had learned to drive by watching him. What Mr. Holmes wanted with them—either Bessie or

Zara would do—didn't give me pause; I was too young to be a Camp Fire Girl; I was just keeping up. I wasn't alarmed by Mr. Holmes—when I cared for a chill, I knew to go to Dr. Fu Manchu, who had his own series in the library. I wasn't fascinated either. There was one thing I wanted from those books, and that was for me to have ten to read at one blow.

Who in the world wrote those books? I knew all the time they were the false "Camp-Fire Girls" and the ones in the library were the authorized. But book reviewers sometimes say of a book that if anyone else had written it, it might not have been this good, and I found it out as a child—their warning is justified. This was a proven case, although a case of the true not being as good as the false. In the true series the characters were either totally different or missing (Mr. Holmes was missing), and there was too much time given to teamwork. The Kress's Campers, besides getting into a more reliable kind of trouble than the Carnegie Campers, had adventures that even they themselves weren't aware of: the pages were in wrong. There were transposed pages, re-peated pages, and whole sections in upside down. There was no way of telling if there was anything missing. But if you knew your way in the woods at all you could enjoy yourself tracking it down. I read the library "Camp Fire Girls," since that's what they were there for, for though they could be read by poorer light they were not as good.

And yet, in a way, the false Campers were no better either. I wonder whether I felt some flaw at the heart of things or whether I was just tired of not having any taste; but it seemed to me when I had finished that the last nine of those books weren't as good as the first one. And the same went for all series books. As long as they are keeping a series going, I was afraid, nothing can really happen. The whole thing is one grand prevention. For my greed, I might have unwittingly dealt with myself in the same way Maria Edgeworth dealt with the one who put her all into the purple jar—I had received word it was just colored water. And my feet hurt too, now and again, from keeping up. That would not have been a good time for me to start in on *Pamela*.

At the Istrione, our movie house, known as the Eye-Strain, stuck in the midst of little girls' "picture-show parties"—we nested in the box—I still enjoyed transposing the Camp Fire Girls into whatever was going on, on the screen. They were in *Drums of Jeopardy* with Alice Brady and *Always Audacious* with Wallace Reid, and anything else we managed to see. Their role—escaping—fitted in anywhere. What those characters always were was dramatic. Of course, the best thing would have been for them to have had a whole picture to themselves. I wanted Marguerite Clark as Bessie, Mae Marsh as Zara and Theodore Roberts as Mr. Holmes—for, should the conclusion ever come (series books try not to think of that, but I always remembered what a difference in *The Lucky Stone* a conclusion would have made), I saw no reason why crusty old Mr. Theodore Roberts Holmes wouldn't give both girls a guinea (close-up here), for they had let him catch them, and then they'd all bounce giggling into one another's arms and the picture could say "The End" and the comedy could start.

And then I found it was nice to come home and read *A Christmas Carol*.

From "A Sweet Devouring," Mademoiselle, 1957

Dylan Thomas
1914–1953

 YLAN THOMAS'S FATHER *was the English mas-*
ter at the grammar school in the Welsh seaport
of Swansea where the poet was born. As a
youngster, Dylan was "small, thin, indecisively
active, quick to get dirty, curly," as he had described himself,
and showed a remarkable talent for poetry. After completing
school, he devoted himself to writing while holding a variety
of odd jobs, including acting, book reviewing and scriptwrit-
ing. He made three cross-country reading tours of the United
States in the 1950's before dying in New York at
the age of thirty-nine.

The first poems I knew were nursery rhymes, and before I
could read them for myself I had come to love just the words
of them, the words alone. What the words stood for, sym-
bolized, or meant, was of very secondary importance; what
mattered was the *sound* of them as I heard them for the first
time on the lips of the remote and incomprehensible grown-
ups who seemed, for some reason, to be living in my world.
And these words were, to me, as the notes of bells, the sounds
of musical instruments, the noises of wind, sea, and rain, the
rattle of milkcarts, the clopping of hooves on cobbles, the
fingering of branches on a window pane, might be to someone, deaf from birth, who has miraculously found his hearing. I did not care what the words said, overmuch, nor what
happened to Jack and Jill and the Mother Goose rest of them;
I cared for the shapes of sound that their names, and the

Dylan Thomas

words describing their actions, made in my ears; I cared for
the colours the words cast on my eyes . . . I fell in love—
that is the only expression I can think of—at once, and am
still at the mercy of words, though, sometimes now, knowing a little of their behaviour very well, I think I can influence
them slightly and have even learned to beat them now and
then, which they appear to enjoy. I tumbled for words at
once. And, when I began to read the nursery rhymes for
myself, and, later, to read other verses and ballads, I knew
that I had discovered the most important things, to me, that
could be ever. There they were, seemingly lifeless, made only
of black and white, but out of them, out of their own being,
came love and terror and pity and pain and wonder and all
the other vague abstractions that make our ephemeral lives
dangerous, great, and bearable. Out of them came the gusts
and grunts and hiccups and hee-haws of the common fun of
the earth; and though what the words meant was, in its own
way, often deliciously funny enough, so much funnier
seemed to me, at that almost forgotten time, the shape and
shade and size and noise of the words as they hummed,
strummed, jigged and galloped along. That was the time of
innocence; words burst upon me, unencumbered by trivial
or portentous association; words were their spring-like
selves, fresh with Eden's dew, as they flew out of the air.
They made their own original associations as they sprung
and shone. The words "Ride a cock-horse to Banbury Cross"
were as haunting to me, who did not know then what a
cock-horse was nor cared a damn where Banbury Cross
might be, as, much later, were such lines as John Donne's
"Go and catch a falling star, Get with child a mandrake root,"
which also I could not understand when I first read them.
And as I read more and more, and it was not all verse, by
any means, my love for the real life of words increased until
I knew that I must live *with* them and in them, always. I

knew, in fact, that I must be a writer of words, and nothing else. The first thing was to feel and know their sound and substance; what I was going to do with those words, what use I was going to make of them, what I was going to *say* through them, would come later. I knew I had to know them most intimately in all their forms and moods, their ups and downs, their chops and changes, their needs and demands.

From "Poetic Manifesto," *The Texas Quarterly*, 1961

Harper Lee
1926–

UCH OF *Harper Lee's best-selling novel* To Kill a Mockingbird *(1960), set in a small southern town during the 1930's, is based on her own childhood in Monroeville, Alabama. Like the six-year-old narrator, Jean Louis ("Scout") Finch, she was the daughter of a lawyer and went on to study law herself at the University of Alabama.* Mockingbird, *the only book published by Lee, was awarded the Pulitzer Prize for fiction and made into a popular film.*

Miss Caroline began the day by reading us a story about cats. The cats had long conversations with one another, they wore cunning little clothes and lived in a warm house beneath a kitchen stove. By the time Mrs. Cat called the drugstore for an order of chocolate malted mice the class was wriggling like a bucketful of catawba worms. Miss Caroline seemed unaware that the ragged, denim-shirted and floursack-skirted first grade, most of whom had chopped cotton and fed hogs from the time they were able to walk, were immune to imaginative literature. Miss Caroline came to the end of the story and said, "*Oh*, my, wasn't that nice?"

Then she went to the blackboard and printed the alphabet in enormous square capitals, turned to the class and asked, "Does anybody know what these are?"

Everybody did; most of the first grade had failed it last year.

I suppose she chose me because she knew my name; as I

Arkansas, 1938.
A typical schoolroom Harper Lee might have known.

read the alphabet a faint line appeared between her eyebrows, and after making me read most of *My First Reader* and the stock-market quotations from *The Mobile Register* aloud, she discovered that I was literate and looked at me with more than faint distaste. Miss Caroline told me to tell my father not to teach me any more, it would interfere with my reading.

"Teach me?" I said in surprise. "He hasn't taught me anything, Miss Caroline. Atticus ain't got time to teach me anything," I added, when Miss Caroline smiled and shook her head. "Why, he's so tired at night he just sits in the livingroom and reads."

"If he didn't teach you, who did?" Miss Caroline asked good-naturedly. "Somebody did. You weren't born reading *The Mobile Register*."

"Jem says I was. He read in a book where I was a Bullfinch instead of a Finch. Jem says my name's really Jean Louise Bullfinch, that I got swapped when I was born and I'm really a—"

Miss Caroline apparently thought I was lying. "Let's not let our imaginations run away with us, dear," she said. "Now you tell your father not to teach you any more. It's best to begin reading with a fresh mind. You tell him I'll take over from here and try to undo the damage—"

"Ma'am?"

"Your father does not know how to teach. You can have a seat now."

I mumbled that I was sorry and retired meditating upon my crime. I never deliberately learned to read, but somehow I had been wallowing illicitly in the daily papers. In the long hours of church—was it then I learned? I could not remember not being able to read hymns. Now that I was compelled to think about it, reading was something that just came to me, as learning to fasten the seat of my union suit without looking around, or achieving two bows from a snarl of shoelaces. I could not remember when the lines above Atticus's moving finger separated into words, but I had stared at them all the evenings of my memory, listening to the news of the day, Bills To Be Enacted into Laws, the diaries of Lorenzo Dow—anything Atticus happened to be reading when I crawled into his lap every night. Until I feared I would lose it, I never loved to read. One does not love breathing.

From *To Kill a Mockingbird*, 1960

Paule Marshall

1929–

HE DAUGHTER *of immigrants from the West Indian island of Barbados who settled in Brooklyn, New York, Paule Marshall has traced her early love of language to hearing the endless, passionate talk of her mother and her mother's friends—"poets in the kitchen" as she called them:*

> *I was that little girl, sitting in the corner of the kitchen, in the company of poets. I was there, seen but not heard, while these marvelous poets carried on. And from way back I always wanted to see if I might not be able to have some of the same power they had with words—their wonderful oral art. I wondered if I could capture some of the same power on paper.*

Marshall's desire to write was enhanced by her discovery of the body of material by black writers and that "maybe there was something important and valid and sacred about that experience of being both Afro-American and West Indian."
Her novels, like this essay, successfully capture that experience.

By the time I was eight or nine, I graduated from the corner of the kitchen to the neighborhood library, and thus from the spoken to the written word. The Macon Street Branch of the Brooklyn Public Library was an imposing half block long edifice of heavy gray masonry, with glass-paneled doors

Paule Marshall

at the front and two tall metal torches symbolizing the light that comes of learning flanking the wide steps.

The inside was just as impressive. More steps—of pale marble with gleaming brass railings at the center and sides—led up to the circulation desk, and a great pendulum clock gazed down from the balcony stacks that faced the entrance. Usually stationed at the top of the steps like the guards outside Buckingham Palace was the custodian, a stern-faced West Indian type who for years, until I was old enough to obtain an adult card, would immediately shoo me with one hand into the Children's Room and with the other threaten me into silence, a finger to his lips. You would have thought he was the chief librarian and not just someone whose job it was to keep the brass polished and the clock wound. I put him in a story called "Barbados" years later and had terrible things happen to him at the end.

I was sheltered from the storm of adolescence in the Macon Street library, reading voraciously, indiscriminately, everything from Jane Austen to Zane Grey, but with a special passion for the long, full-blown, richly detailed eighteenth- and nineteenth-century picaresque tales: *Tom Jones, Great Expectations, Vanity Fair.*

But although I loved nearly everything I read and would enter full into the lives of the characters—indeed, would cease being myself and become them—I sensed a lack after a time. Something I couldn't quite define was missing. And then one day, browsing in the poetry section, I came across a book by someone called Paul Laurence Dunbar, and opening it, I found the photograph of a wistful, sad-eyed poet who to my surprise was black. I turned to a poem at random. "Little brown-baby wif spa'klin'/eyes/Come to yo' pappy an' set on his knee." Although I had a little difficulty at first with the words in dialect, the poem spoke to me as nothing I had read before of the closeness, the special relationship I had had with my father, who by then had become an ardent believer in Father Divine and gone to live in Father's "kingdom" in Harlem. Reading it helped to ease somewhat the tight knot of sorrow and longing I carried around in my chest that refused to go away. I read another poem: "Lias! Lias! Bless de Lawd!/Don' you know de day's/erbroad?/Ef you don' get up, you scamp/Dey'll be trouble in dis camp." I laughed. It reminded me of the way my mother sometimes yelled at my sister and me to get out of bed in the mornings.

And another: "Seen my lady home las' night/Jump back, honey, jump back./Hel' huh han' an' sque'z it tight . . ." About love between a black man and a black woman. I had never seen that written about before and it roused in me all kinds of delicious feelings and hopes.

And I began to search then for books and stories and poems about "The Race" (as it was put back then), about my people. While not abandoning Thackeray, Fielding, Dickens and the others, I started asking the reference librarian, who was white, for books by Negro writers, although I must admit I did so at first with a feeling of shame—the shame I and many others used to experience in those days whenever the word "Negro" or "colored" came up.

No grade school literature teacher of mine had ever mentioned Dunbar or James Weldon Johnson or Langston Hughes. I didn't know that Zora Neale Hurston existed and was busy writing and being published during those years. Nor was I made aware of people like Frederick Douglass and Harriet Tubman—their spirit and example—or the great nineteenth-century abolitionist and feminist Sojourner Truth. There wasn't even Negro History Week when I attended P.S. 35 on Decatur Street!

. . . It was around that time also that I began harboring the dangerous thought of someday trying to write myself. Perhaps a poem about an apple tree, although I had never

seen one. Or the story of a girl who could magically trans-
plant herself to wherever she wanted to be in the world—
such as Father Divine's kingdom in Harlem. Dunbar—his
dark, eloquent face, his large volume of poems—permitted
me to dream that I might someday write, and with something
of the power with words my mother and her friends possessed. . . .

From "From the Poets in the Kitchen,"
The New York Times Book Review, January 9, 1983

Richard Rodriguez

Richard Rodriguez
1944–

ICHARD RODRIGUEZ'S PARENTS, *both natives of Mexico, spoke only Spanish in their home in Sacramento, California, while he was growing up. When he began his schooling, Rodriguez knew only fifty words of English. In his intellectual autobiography,* Hunger of Memory *(1982), he has poignantly recorded his journey from a "socially disadvantaged" child to a successful writer and lecturer with degrees from Stanford and Columbia, and remembers the pleasures of reading as a nine-year-old.*

In fourth grade I embarked upon a grandiose reading program. "Give me the names of important books," I would say to startled teachers. They soon found out that I had in mind "adult books." I ignored their suggestion of anything I suspected was written for children (Not until I was in college, as a result, did I read *Huckleberry Finn* or *Alice's Adventures in Wonderland.*) Instead, I read *The Scarlet Letter* and Franklin's *Autobiography.* And whatever I read I read for extra credit. Each time I finished a book, I reported the achievement to a teacher and basked in the praise my effort earned. Despite my best efforts, however, there seemed to be more and more books I needed to read. At the library I would literally tremble as I came upon whole shelves of books I hadn't read. So I read and I read and I read: *Great Expectations*; all the short stories of Kipling; *The Babe Ruth Story*; the entire first volume of the *Encyclopaedia Britannica*

(A-ANSTEY); the Iliad; Moby Dick; Gone with the Wind; The Good Earth; Ramona; Forever Amber; The Lives of the Saints; Crime and Punishment; The Pearl. . . . Librarians who initially frowned when I checked out the maximum ten books at a time started saving books they thought I might like. Teachers would say to the rest of the class, "I only wish the rest of you took reading as seriously as Richard obviously does."

But at home I would hear my mother wondering, "What do you see in your books?" (Was reading a hobby like her knitting? Was so much reading even healthy for a boy? Was it the sign of "brains?" Or was it just a convenient excuse for not helping around the house on Saturday mornings?) Always, "What do you see. . . . ?"

. . . In spite of my earnestness, I found reading a pleasurable activity. I came to enjoy the lonely good company of books. Early on weekday mornings, I'd read in my bed. I'd feel a mysterious comfort then, reading in the dawn quiet— the blue-gray silence interrupted by the occasional churning of the refrigerator motor a few rooms away or the more distant sounds of a city bus beginning its run. On weekends I'd go to the public library to read, surrounded by old men and women. Or, if the weather was fine, I would take my books to the park and read in the shade of a tree. A warm summer evening was my favorite reading time. Neighbors would leave for vacation and I would water their lawns. I would sit through the twilight on the front porches or in backyards, reading to the cool, whirling sounds of the sprinklers.

From *Hunger of Memory; The Education of Richard Rodriguez,* 1981

Stephen King
1947–

TEPHEN KING'S SUCCESS as a novelist may be unrivaled in modern publishing history. Few writers have reached sales figures of over 25 million books, and none save King have staked a solid claim as the undisputed master of a very special literary genre—the horror story. Since the appearance of Carrie *in 1974, it seems that the best-seller list has always included a novel by King. He was born in Maine and raised by his mother after his father—"a man with an itchy foot," as King described him—deserted them in 1949. After living in different parts of the country, they settled in Durham, Maine, when King was eleven. It was then that he discovered fantasy horror fiction.*

About a quarter of a mile away from the small house in Durham where my brother and I finished our growing up, there was a lovely brick house where my mother's sister, Ethelyn Pillsbury Flaws, and her husband, Oren, lived. Over the Flaws's garage was a lovely, long attic room with loose, rumbling boards and that entrancing attic smell.

At that time the attic connected with a whole complex of outbuildings, which in turn finally led to a great old barn—all of these buildings smelling intoxicatingly of sweet hay long departed. But there was a reminder of the days when animals had been kept in the barn. If one climbed to the third loft, one could observe the skeletons of several chickens that had apparently died of some strange disease up there. It was

Stephen King

a pilgrimage I made often; there was something fascinating about those chicken skeletons, lying in a drift of feathers as ephemeral as moondust, some secret in the black sockets where their eyes had once been. . . .

But the attic over the garage was a kind of family museum. Everyone on the Pillsbury side of the family had stored things up there from time to time, from furniture to photographs, and there was just room for a small boy to twist and turn his way along narrow aisles, ducking under the arm of a standing lamp or stepping over a crate of old wallpaper samples that someone had wanted saved for some forgotten reason.

My brother and I were not actually forbidden the attic, but my Aunt Ethelyn frowned on our visits up there because the floorboards had only been laid, not nailed, and some were missing. It would have been easy enough, I suppose, to trip and go headfirst through a hole and down to the concrete floor below—or into the bed of my Uncle Oren's green Chevy pickup truck.

For me, on a cold fall day in 1959 or 1960, the attic over my aunt and uncle's garage was the place where that interior dowsing rod suddenly turned over, where the compass needle swung emphatically toward some mental true north. That was the day I happened to come on a box of my father's books . . . paperbacks from the mid-forties.

There was a lot of my mother and father's married life in the attic, and I can understand how, in the wake of his sudden disappearance from her life, she would want to take as many of his things as possible and put them away in a dark place. It was there, a year or two earlier, that my brother found a reel of movie film my father had taken on shipboard. Dave and I pooled some money we had saved (without my mother's knowledge), rented a movie projector, and watched it over and over again in fascinated silence. My father turned the camera over to someone else at one point and there he is, Donald King of Peru, Indiana, standing against the rail. He raises his hand; smiles; unknowingly waves to sons who were then not even conceived. We rewound it, watched it, rewound it, watched it again. And again. Hi, Dad; wonder where you are now.

In another box there were piles of his merchant marine manuals; in another, scrapbooks of stuff from foreign countries. My mother told me that while he would go around with a paperback western stuffed into his back pocket, his real interest was in science fiction and horror stories. He tried his own hand at a number of tales of this type, submitting them to the popular men's magazines of the day, *Bluebook* and *Argosy* among them. He ultimately published nothing ("Your father didn't have a great deal of stick-to-it in his nature," my mother once told me dryly, and that was about as close as she ever came to ranking him out), but he did get several personal rejection notes; "This-won't-do-but-send-us-more" notes I used to call them in my teens and early twenties, when I collected a good many of my own (during periods of depression I would sometimes wonder what it would be like to blow your nose on a rejection slip).

The box I found that day was a treasure trove of old Avon paperbacks. Avon, in those days, was the one paperback publisher committed to fantasy and weird fiction. I remember those books with great affection—particularly the shiny over-coating which all Avons bore, a material that was a cross betwen isinglass and Saran Wrap. When and if the story lagged, you could peel this shiny stuff off the cover in long strips. It made a perfectly wonderful noise. And although it wanders from the subject, I also remember the forties Dell paperbacks with love—they were all mysteries back then, and on the back of each was a luxurious map showing the scene of the crime.

One of those books was an Avon "sampler"—the word *anthology* was apparently considered too esoteric for readers of this sort of material to grasp. It contained stories by Frank Belknap Long ("The Hounds of Tindalos"), Zelia Bishop ("The Curse of Yig"), and a host of other tales culled from the early days of *Weird Tales* magazine. Two of the others were novels by A. Merritt—*Burn, Witch, Burn* (not to be confused with the later Fritz Leiber novel, *Conjure Wife*) and *The Metal Monster*.

The pick of the litter, however, was an H. P. Lovecraft collection from 1947 called *The Lurking Fear and Other Stories*. I remember the picture on the cover very well: a cemetery (somewhere near Providence, one assumes!) at night, and coming out from beneath a tombstone, a loathsome green thing with long fangs and burning red eyes. Behind it, suggested but not graphically drawn, was a tunnel leading down into the bowels of the earth. Since then I've seen literally hundreds of editions of Lovecraft, yet that remains the one which best sums up H. P. L.'s work for me . . . and I've no idea who the artist might have been.

From: *Danse Macabre*, 1981

Annie Dillard with her father

Annie Dillard
1945–

A POET *and walker with a background in theology and a penchant for quirky facts" is how Annie Dillard once described herself. However, it was not for her poetry, but for her first published prose work,* Pilgrim at Tinker Creek *(1974), that the Pittsburgh-born writer won national recognition. This beautiful book of mystical excursions in the Roanoke Valley of Virginia was awarded a Pulitzer Prize. Books of poetry, travel, and autobiography have followed.*

It was clear that adults, including our parents, approved of children who read books, but it was not at all clear why this was so. Our reading was subversive, and we knew it. Did they think we read to improve our vocabularies? Did they want us to read and not pay the least bit of heed to what we read, as they wanted us to go to Sunday school and ignore what we heard?

I was now believing books more than I believed what I saw and heard. I was reading books about the actual, historical, moral world—in which somehow I felt I was not living.

The French and Indian War had been, for me, a purely literary event. Skilled men in books could survive it. Those who died, an arrow through the heart, thrilled me by their last words. This recent war's survivors, some still shaking, some still in mourning, taught in our classrooms. "*Wir waren asugebommt,*" one dear old white-haired Polish lady related in German class, her family was "bombed out," and we laughed, we smart girls, because this was our slang for "drunk." Those who died in this war's books died whether they were skilled or not. Bombs fell on their cities or ships, or they starved in the camps or were gassed or shot, or they stepped on land mines and died surprised, trying to push their intestines back in their abdomens with their fingers and thumbs.

What I sought in books was imagination. It was depth, depth of thought and feeling; some sort of extreme of subject matter; some nearness to death; some call to courage. I myself was getting wild; I wanted wildness, originality, genius, rapture, hope. I wanted strength, not tea parties. What I sought in books was a world whose surfaces, whose people and events and days lived, actually matched the exaltation of the interior life. There you could live.

Those of us who read carried around with us like martyrs a secret knowledge, a secret joy, and a secret hope: There is a life worth living where history is still taking place; there are ideas worth dying for, and circumstances where courage is still prized. This life could be found and joined, like the Resistance. I kept this exhilarating faith alive in myself, concealed under my uniform shirt like an oblate's ribbon; I would not be parted from it.

From *An American Childhood*, 1987

Afterword

Is there a "community of the book?" The Center for the Book in the Library of Congress was established in 1977 on the assumption that such a community exists and that it can be mobilized to keep books and reading central to our personal lives and to the life of our democracy. A national partnership between the Library of Congress and private citizens and organizations, the Center for the Book's purpose is to stimulate public interest in books, reading, and libraries.

The most important person in this partnership or community is the individual reader. Former Librarian of Congress Daniel J. Boorstin, the Center's founder, emphasized this point when the Center was created: "As the national library of a great free republic, the Library of Congress has a special duty and a special interest to see that books do not go unread . . . here we shape plans for a grand national effort to make all our people eager, avid, understanding, critical readers." In "A Nation of Readers," a talk presented in 1982, Boorstin explained how our country was built on books and reading. We can become A Nation of Readers once again, he asserted, if our citizens and institutions will make a new commitment to keeping "the culture of the book" alive. In this effort, which is a basic mission of The Center for the Book, technology is an ally. As Boorstin explained, "We have a special duty to see that the book is the useful, illuminating servant of all other technologies, and that all other technologies become the effective, illuminating acolytes of the book."

The Center for the Book seeks not only to help keep this country's book culture alive, but also to help it flourish. We are always looking for innovative ways to expand the audience for books and reading. In this effort technology indeed has proven to be an ally, for the Center has developed reading promotion projects with five national television networks. The best known network effort is the Library of Congress/ CBS Television "Read More About It" book project, a series of thirty-second reading messages following major CBS television programs that send viewers to their local libraries or bookstores to read more about the subject of the program. However, the center's most effective means of involving other organizations and individuals in its activities has been through the use of broad reading promotion themes such as "A Nation of Readers," "Read More About It," "Books Make a Difference," and, most popular of all, "1989—The Year of the Young Reader."

Official support for the "1989—The Year of the Young Reader" campaign has come from Congress, the President, and from governors and mayors throughout the country. Dr. James H. Billington, the Librarian of Congress, enlisted the help of First Lady Barbara Bush, who is honorary chairperson of the Year of the Young Reader campaign. In this capacity Mrs. Bush, a longtime supporter of literacy and reading projects, is making visits around the country on behalf of local literacy projects and Year of the Young Reader events.

Over thirty American publishers are participating in the Year of the Young Reader campaign through their own projects or tax-deductible contributions to the Center for the Book to support projects around the country. Major organizational partners include the American Booksellers Association, the American Library Association, the Association of Booksellers for Children, the Children's Book Council, and Reading is Fundamental, Inc. The nineteen statewide centers for the book, each affiliated with The Center for the Book in the Library of Congress, are sponsoring Year of the Young Reader projects and activities.

Steven Gilbar's THE OPEN DOOR: WHEN WRITERS FIRST LEARNED TO READ brings us to the heart of the relationship between books and young readers. Books and reading change lives, especially young lives. These marvelous examples, drawn from authors who themselves changed lives through their own writings, enlighten and inspire our efforts. The Center for the Book is grateful to Steven Gilbar for contributing his royalties from this book to the Year of the Young Reader campaign.

John Y. Cole, Director
The Center for the Book in the Library of Congress

Bibliography

ANDERSON, SHERWOOD. *Sherwood Anderson's Memoirs.* New York: Harcourt, Brace and Company, 1942. 57, 60.

CAHAN, ABRAHAM. *The Rise of David Levinsky.* New York: Harper and Brothers, 1960. 138–139.

CHURCHILL, WINSTON S. *My Early Life: A Roving Commission.* New York: Charles Scribner's Sons, 1930. 3–4.

COBBETT, WILLIAM. *The Autobiography of William Cobbett: The Progress of a Plough-Boy to a Seat in Parliament.* ed. William Reitzel. London: Faber and Faber Limited. 1947. 18–19.

CUMMINGS, E. E. *i: six nonlectures.* New York: Atheneum Press, 1962. 26–28.

DICKENS, CHARLES. *David Copperfield.* New York: Dodd, Mead, and Company, 1943. 53–54.

DILLARD, ANNIE. *An American Childhood.* New York: Harper and Row, 1986. 182–184.

DOUGLASS, FREDERICK. *Life and Times of Frederick Douglass.* Hartford, Connecticut: Park Publishing Company, 1881. 69–71.

DURANT, WILL. *Transition: A Sentimental Story of One Mind and One Era.* New York: Simon and Schuster, 1927. 41–44.

FISHER, M. F. K. *Among Friends.* New York: Alfred A. Knopf, 1971. 265–267.

FRANKLIN, BENJAMIN. *The Autobiography of Benjamin*

Franklin. ed., John Bigelow. New York and London: G. P. Putnam and Sons, 1868. 20–23.

KING, STEPHEN. *Danse Macabre.* New York: Berkley Books, 1981. 93–96.

KIPLING, RUDYARD. *Something of Myself: For My Friends Known and Unknown.* London: Macmillan and Company, Ltd., 1951. 6–9.

LEE, HARPER. *To Kill a Mockingbird.* Philadelphia and New York: J. B. Lippincott Company, 1960. 23–24.

LEWIS, C. S. *Surprised by Joy: The Shape of My Early Life.* New York: Harcourt, Brace and Company, 1955. 10, 14–15.

MARSHALL, PAULE. "From the Poets in the Kitchen." *The New York Times Book Review* (January 9, 1983): 34–35.

MENCKEN, H. L. *Happy Days: 1880–1892.* New York: Alfred A. Knopf, 1940. 157–159.

MILNE, A. A. *Autobiography.* New York: E. P. Dutton and Company, Inc., 1939. 44–45.

RHYS, JEAN. *Smile Please: An Unfinished Autobiography.* New York: Harper and Row, Publishers, 1979. 20–21.

RODRIGUEZ, RICHARD. *Hunger of Memory: The Education of Richard Rodriguez.* Boston: David R. Godine, Publisher, Inc., 1981. 61–63.

SINCLAIR, UPTON. *The Autobiography of Upton Sinclair.* New York: Harcourt, Brace and World Inc., 1962. 8–9.

SINGER, ISAAC BASHEVIS, and Moskowitz, Ira. *A Little Boy in Search of God: Mysticism in a Personal Light.* Garden

City, New York: Doubleday and Company, Inc., 1976.
75–85.

STEIN, GERTRUDE. *The Autobiography of Alice B. Toklas.*
New York: Harcourt, Brace and Company, 1933. 91–92.

STEINBECK, JOHN. *The Acts of King Arthur and His Noble
Knights: From the Winchester Manuscripts of Thomas Malory
and Other Sources.* ed., Chase Horton. New York: Ballan-
tine Books, 1976. 3–5.

THOMAS, DYLAN. "Poetic Manifesto." *Texas Quarterly* 4
(Winter 1961): 45–46.

WELLS, H. G. *Experiment in Autobiography: Discoveries and
Conclusions of a Very Ordinary Brain.* New York: The Macmillan Company, 1934. 53–55.

WELTY, EUDORA. "A Sweet Devouring." *Mademoiselle*
(December 1957): 49, 114–116.

WRIGHT, RICHARD. *Black Boy: A Record of Childhood and
Youth.* New York: Harper and Row, Publishers, 1945.
271–276.

YEATS, WILLIAM BUTLER. *Reveries Over Childhood and
Youth.* Churchtown, Dundrum: The Cuala Press, 1971. 23–
26, 50–52.

Permissions

THE OPEN DOOR

was set on the Linotron 202 in Bembo, a design based on
the types used by Venetian scholar-publisher Aldus Manutius
in the printing of *De Aetna*, written by Pietro Bembo and
published in 1495. The original characters were cut in 1490
by Francesco Griffo who, at Aldus's request, later cut the
first italic types. Originally adapted by the English Monotype
Company, Bembo is now widely available and highly
regarded. It remains one of the most elegant, readable,
and widely used of all book faces.

Composed by DEKR Corporation, Woburn, Massachusetts.
Printed and bound by Arcata Graphics—Halliday,
West Hanover, Massachusetts.
Designed by Lisa Clark.